ENGLISH
FOR EVERYONE
ENGLISH IDIOMS

FREE AUDIO
website and app
www.dkefe.com

Author

Thomas Booth worked for 10 years as an English-language teacher in Poland and Russia. He now lives in England, where he works as an editor and English-language materials writer. He has contributed to a number of books in the *English for Everyone* series.

US consultant

Jenny Wilson, MEd, has taught English as a foreign language in the US and UK for many years, at private institutes and universities including the University of Wisconsin–Madison. She has also worked as an IELTS examiner and written English-language materials for Collins Language, Cambridge University Press, and Corwin.

ENGLISH FOR EVERYONE

ENGLISH IDIOMS

DK

DK Penguin Random House

US Editor Kayla Dugger
Senior Editor Laura Sandford
Senior Art Editor Amy Child
Illustration Square Egg
Managing Editor Christine Stroyan
Managing Art Editor Anna Hall
Jacket Designer Surabhi Wadhwa
Jacket Editor Emma Dawson
Jacket Design Development Manager Sophia MTT
Producer, Pre-production Robert Dunn
Producer Jude Crozier
Publisher Andrew Macintyre
Art Director Karen Self
Publishing Director Jonathan Metcalf

DK India
Senior Editor Janashree Singha
Assistant Editor Rishi Bryan
Project Art Editor Vikas Sachdeva
Art Editors Pallavi Kapur, Roshni Kapur
Assistant Art Editor Monam Nishat
Managing Editor Soma B. Chowdhury
Senior Managing Art Editor Arunesh Talapatra
Pre-production Manager Balwant Singh
DTP Designer Anita Yadav

First American Edition, 2019
Published in the United States by DK Publishing,
a division of Penguin Random House LLC
1745 Broadway, 20th Floor, New York, NY 10019

25 10 9 8 7 6 5 4 3
003–334973–Feb/2023

Published in Great Britain by Dorling Kindersley Limited

A catalog record for this book
is available from the Library of Congress.
Box set ISBN 978-0-7440-8186-2
ISBN 978-1-4654-8040-8

Printed and bound in China

www.dk.com

MIX Paper | Supporting responsible forestry FSC™ C018179 www.fsc.org

This book was made with Forest Stewardship Council™ certified paper—one small step in DK's commitment to a sustainable future.
Learn more at www.dk.com/uk/information/sustainability

Contents

COMMUNICATION

EVERYDAY LIFE

WORK AND ACHIEVEMENTS

EXPRESSIONS

How to use this book

English for Everyone: English Idioms will help you learn, understand, and remember the most common English idioms and expressions. Each of the 54 units in the book consists of a teaching spread on a subject or theme, with illustrated sentences to place the idiom in context, and then a practice spread with exercises to reinforce what you have learned. Listen to the free audio and repeat each expression and sentence. The answers to all the exercises are at the back of the book, along with comprehensive indexes.

Unit number The book is divided into units. The unit number helps you keep track of your progress.

Modules Many teaching spreads are broken into modules covering different categories of idioms.

Module number Every module is identified with a unique number, so you can easily locate the related audio.

Sample sentences English idioms are shown in the context of a sample sentence.

Definitions Idiomatic English expressions are accompanied by definitions.

Supporting graphics Visual cues help you understand and remember new idioms.

Write-on lines You are encouraged to write your own translations of English idioms to create your own reference pages.

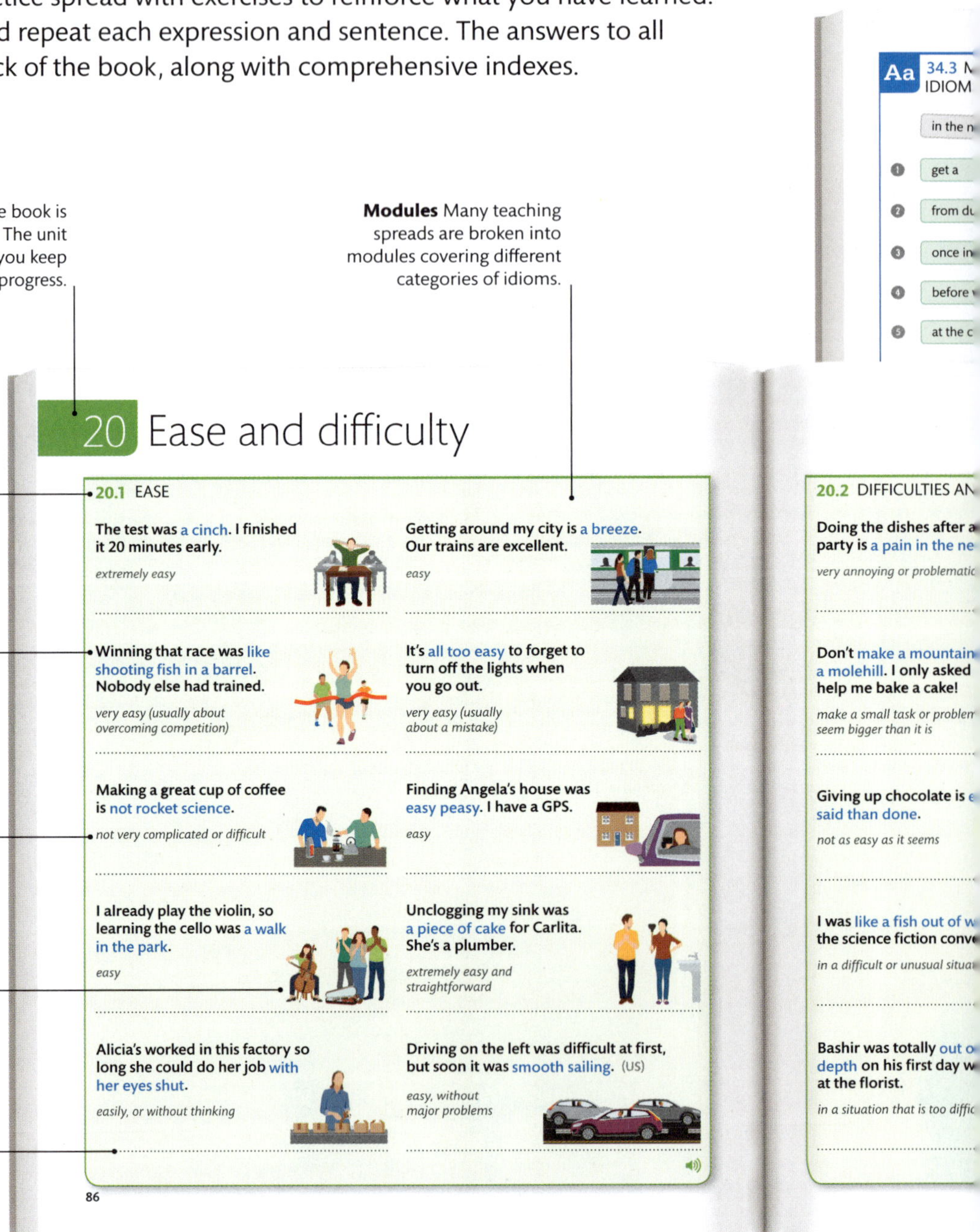

20 Ease and difficulty

20.1 EASE

The test was a cinch. I finished it 20 minutes early.
extremely easy

Getting around my city is a breeze. Our trains are excellent.
easy

Winning that race was like shooting fish in a barrel. Nobody else had trained.
very easy (usually about overcoming competition)

It's all too easy to forget to turn off the lights when you go out.
very easy (usually about a mistake)

Making a great cup of coffee is not rocket science.
not very complicated or difficult

Finding Angela's house was easy peasy. I have a GPS.
easy

I already play the violin, so learning the cello was a walk in the park.
easy

Unclogging my sink was a piece of cake for Carlita. She's a plumber.
extremely easy and straightforward

Alicia's worked in this factory so long she could do her job with her eyes shut.
easily, or without thinking

Driving on the left was difficult at first, but soon it was smooth sailing. (US)
easy, without major problems

86

TEACHING SPREAD

Listening exercise This symbol indicates that you should listen to an audio track in order to answer the questions in the exercise.

Exercise number Each exercise is identified with a unique number, so you can easily locate answers.

Sample answer The first question of each exercise is answered for you, to help make the task easy to understand.

Exercise instruction Each exercise is introduced with a brief instruction, telling you what you need to do.

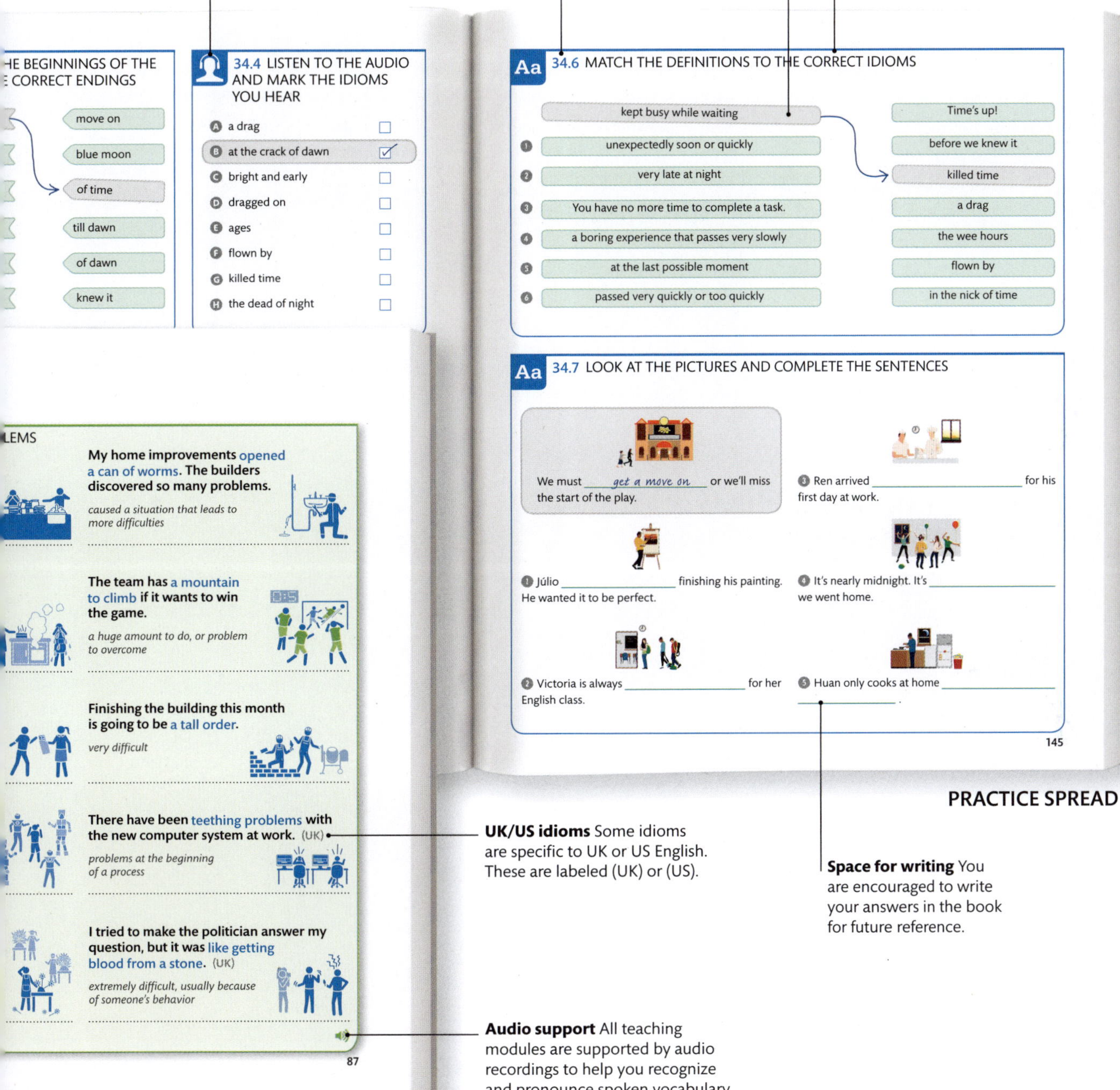

…HE BEGINNINGS OF THE …E CORRECT ENDINGS

move on / blue moon / of time / till dawn / of dawn / knew it

34.4 LISTEN TO THE AUDIO AND MARK THE IDIOMS YOU HEAR

- A a drag ☐
- B at the crack of dawn ☑
- C bright and early ☐
- D dragged on ☐
- E ages ☐
- F flown by ☐
- G killed time ☐
- H the dead of night ☐

Aa 34.6 MATCH THE DEFINITIONS TO THE CORRECT IDIOMS

kept busy while waiting	Time's up!
1 unexpectedly soon or quickly	before we knew it
2 very late at night	killed time
3 You have no more time to complete a task.	a drag
4 a boring experience that passes very slowly	the wee hours
5 at the last possible moment	flown by
6 passed very quickly or too quickly	in the nick of time

Aa 34.7 LOOK AT THE PICTURES AND COMPLETE THE SENTENCES

We must *get a move on* or we'll miss the start of the play.

1 Júlio ______ finishing his painting. He wanted it to be perfect.

2 Victoria is always ______ for her English class.

3 Ren arrived ______ for his first day at work.

4 It's nearly midnight. It's ______ we went home.

5 Huan only cooks at home ______.

145

…LEMS

My home improvements opened a can of worms. The builders discovered so many problems.
caused a situation that leads to more difficulties

The team has a mountain to climb if it wants to win the game.
a huge amount to do, or problem to overcome

Finishing the building this month is going to be a tall order.
very difficult

There have been teething problems with the new computer system at work. (UK)
problems at the beginning of a process

I tried to make the politician answer my question, but it was like getting blood from a stone. (UK)
extremely difficult, usually because of someone's behavior

87

PRACTICE SPREAD

UK/US idioms Some idioms are specific to UK or US English. These are labeled (UK) or (US).

Space for writing You are encouraged to write your answers in the book for future reference.

Audio support All teaching modules are supported by audio recordings to help you recognize and pronounce spoken vocabulary.

Idioms and expressions

Idioms can be one of the most difficult parts of a language for learners to understand and use correctly. *English for Everyone: English Idioms* includes over 1,000 of the most common and useful English idioms, along with set expressions and easily confused words.

IDIOMS
Idioms are expressions that cannot be understood literally. For example, "like two peas in a pod" has nothing to do with peas, but means two people look alike.

Idiomatic expression

Mateo and his brother Lucas are like two peas in a pod. I can't tell them apart.

SET EXPRESSIONS
Some of the expressions in this book are not idioms, but particular common combinations of words. Learners often make mistakes when they use these set expressions.

Set expression

Shreya's going to have a baby this summer.

EASILY CONFUSED WORDS
This books also includes two units on words that are easily confused by English-language learners, such as "say" and "tell."

When you use "say", you don't have to state who a person is talking to.

"Oh, no," said Kayleigh. "I've left my school bag on the bus with all my homework in it."

When you use "tell", you must state who a person is talking to.

Kayleigh had to tell her teacher that she had left her homework on the bus.

Audio

English for Everyone: English Idioms features extensive supporting audio resources. Every expression and sentence in the teaching spreads is recorded, and you are encouraged to listen to the audio and repeat the phrases and sentences out loud, until you are confident you understand and can pronounce what has been said.

SUPPORTING AUDIO
This symbol indicates that audio recordings of the idioms and sentences in a module are available for you to listen to.

LISTENING EXERCISES
This symbol indicates that you should listen to an audio track in order to answer the questions in the exercise.

FREE AUDIO
website and app
www.dkefe.com

Answers

The book is designed to make it easy to monitor your progress. Answers are provided for every exercise, so you can see how well you have understood and remembered the idioms and expressions you have learned.

Exercise numbers Match these numbers to the number at the top-left corner of each exercise.

Answers Find the answers to every exercise printed at the back of the book.

36

36.4
1 B 2 A 3 B 4 C

36.5
1 She's working hard.
2 We rested.
3 Julie tried her best.
4 Carmen is not working
5 It was hard work.

36.6
1 Leo always goes the ext customers happy.
2 Akash usually takes 40 his lunch.
3 I'm sorry, I can't talk to hands full.
4 Celia had to put her he essay to meet the deadline
5 Brandon is a slacker. He and ignores the customers
6 After a long day workin to put his feet up and watc

Indexes

This book includes two indexes: an index of idioms and expressions, and an index of common words and subjects.

INDEX OF IDIOMS AND EXPRESSIONS
The index of idioms and expressions contains every expression from the teaching spreads, listed in alphabetical order by key word.

M
can't **make** heads or tails of (US) / can't make head or tail of (UK) 31.1
make a beeline for 37.1
make a cake 43.1
make a choice 43.1
make a fresh start 18.1
make a joke 43.1
make a mess 43.1
make a mountain out of a molehill 20.2
make a noise 43.1
make a phone call 43.1
make a pig's ear of something 7.1
make a rod for your own back 22.2
make arrangements 43.1
make a scene 28.1
make ends meet 32.1
make great strides 37.1
make progress 43.1
make some friends 43.1
make someone's blood boil 13.1
make someone's hair stand on end 13.3
make someone's mouth water 29.1
make waves 23.2
keep in **mind** (US) / bear in mind (UK) 14.1
someone's **mind** goes blank 14.1
something slips your **mind** 14.1
speak your **mind** 24.2
spring to **mind** 14.1
great **minds** think alike 31.1
a **minefield** 16.1
a misery guts (UK), *see* a downer (US)
go **missing** 47.1
break the **mold** 31.3
make a mountain out of a **molehill** 20.2
easy **money** 32.1
money doesn't grow on trees 32.1
throw **money** around 32.1
throw **money** down the drain 32.1
once in a blue **moon** 34.1, 54.1
over the **moon** 12.1
moth-eaten 6.1
set the wheels in **motion** 37.1
a **mountain** to climb 20.2
make a **mountain** out of a molehill 20.2
as quiet as a **mouse** 50.2
be born with a silver spoon in your **mouth** 3.3
by word of **mouth** 25.1
foam at the **mouth** 11.2

UK/US idioms If an idiom has a UK or US equivalent, both versions are listed in the index.

Key words Each entry in the index contains a key word from the expression in bold.

Module number Match the number in the index to the module number on the teaching page.

INDEX OF COMMON WORDS AND SUBJECTS
Use this index to find idioms relating to a subject or expressions using a common word.

A
"absolutely" 49.1
advantage and disadvantage 3.3
adverbs, intensifying 49
age 1
agreement 9.1
amount 17.1
anger 13.2
animals 4.2, **7**, 25.2, 41.4, 50.2
appearance 3
arts, the 28
"as" 50.1
authority 38

B
background 3.3
bad things 6
"beat" 52.4
beginning 18.1
behavior 10
body, the 11.1, **15**, 38.2
"borrow" 52.5
business 40, 41

01 Age

1.1 IDIOMS ABOUT AGE

After climbing the hill, I realized I'm no spring chicken!

no longer young

My assistant is a bit wet behind the ears. He still has a lot to learn.

young and inexperienced

Becky's worried she's getting on in years after spotting more gray hairs. (US)

getting old

Sanjay feels as old as the hills when his kids talk about technology.

extremely old

These bright young things have just started college.

young, enthusiastic, fashionable, or ambitious people

This TV show bridges the generation gap. The whole family loves it.

appeals to people of all ages

1.2 EXPRESSIONS WITH "AGE"

My grandpa got married again at the ripe old age of 92.

very old age

Brendan's teacher told him to start acting his age.

behaving in a way appropriate to his age

Sally first sang on stage at the tender age of 7.

very young age

I feel my age when I go shopping with my children.

am conscious of being older

I've just turned 40, and I'm in the prime of my life. I always go to the gym after work.

at my best; healthy and successful

Katie started learning piano when she was knee-high to a grasshopper.

very young

I'm too long in the tooth to try out skydiving.

old

Derek and Joan spent their twilight years traveling the world.

the last years of someone's life

I can't come to that nightclub with you! I'm over the hill.

old; past my best years

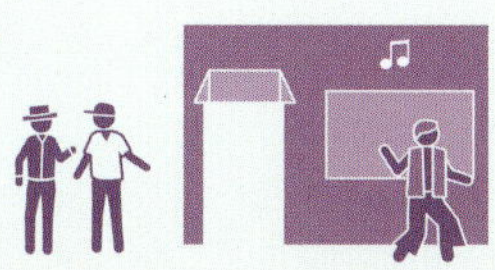

Angela might be 84, but she is still young at heart.

youthful, despite being old

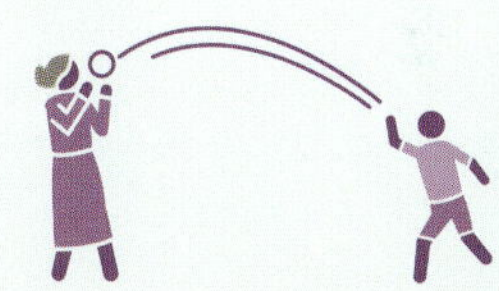

Damien's at that awkward age and finds it hard to talk to people.

the period of adolescence when people feel very self-conscious

In many countries, there is a big celebration when young people come of age.

reach maturity, or have the same legal rights as adults

Many singers' voices improve with age.

get better as they get older

Stephen has reached the great age of 100.

very old age

Aa 1.3 WRITE THE IDIOMS FROM THE PANEL IN THE CORRECT GROUPS

YOUNG	OLD
bright young things	

no spring chicken ~~bright young things~~ tender age

over the hill knee-high to a grasshopper great age

1.4 LISTEN TO THE AUDIO AND COMPLETE THE SENTENCES THAT DESCRIBE EACH PICTURE

I've just turned 40, and I'm in the prime of my life. I always go to the gym after work.

3 My grandpa got married again at the ______________ of 92.

1 Becky's worried she's ______________ after spotting more gray hairs.

4 This TV show ______________ ______________. The whole family loves it.

2 Damien's at ______________ and finds it hard to talk to people.

5 I ______________ when I go shopping with my children.

Aa 1.5 REWRITE THE SENTENCES, CORRECTING THE ERRORS

Brendan's teacher told him to start **playing his age**.
Brendan's teacher told him to start acting his age.

1 I'm too **long in the mouth** to try out skydiving.

2 My assistant is a bit **wet behind the neck**. He still has a lot to learn.

3 Derek and Joan spent their **midnight years** traveling the world.

4 In many countries, there is a big celebration when young people **arrive of age**.

5 Angela might be 84, but she is still **young at mind**.

6 Sanjay feels **as old as the mountains** when his kids talk about technology.

Aa 1.6 WRITE THE CORRECT IDIOM NEXT TO ITS DEFINITION, FILLING IN THE MISSING LETTERS

no longer young = n *o* s *p r i n g* c *h i c k e n*

1 get better as they get older = i _ _ _ _ _ _ w _ _ _ a _ _

2 old; past my best years = o _ _ _ t _ _ h _ _ _

3 very old age = g _ _ _ _ _ a _ _

4 the last years of someone's life = t _ _ _ _ _ _ _ y _ _ _ _

5 youthful, despite being old = y _ _ _ _ a _ h _ _ _ _

6 very young age = t _ _ _ _ _ a _ _

02 Friends and family

2.1 FRIENDSHIP

Harper regrets losing touch with all her old school friends.

no longer being in contact with

I think Claire's found a soulmate. Both she and Dan love reading.

the perfect person to be a friend or partner

I've kept in touch with Lin since we left college 25 years ago.

continued to be in contact with

Marie and Pierre met through Isaac, a mutual friend of theirs.

a shared friend of two people

Ramón and Tara get on like a house on fire. They're always talking and laughing.

get along extremely well; have a very good relationship

Mia and I have drifted apart since she left our choir and started boxing instead.

slowly become less friendly or close to each other

I struck up a friendship with Pete while we were in cooking class last year.

became friends with

My wife and I hit it off immediately when we first met at a country music concert.

became friends very quickly

Donna was a fair-weather friend. She wouldn't help when my house flooded.

a friend who deserts you when you have difficulties

Cy and I got off on the wrong foot on our date. He was an hour late and forgot my name.

started our relationship badly

2.2 FAMILY

Bob reminds me so much of his father. He is a chip off the old block.

very similar to someone in his family

Jade is a family friend. She grew up on the same street as us.

someone who has known your family for some time

Uncle Tony is the black sheep of the family. He's been to prison three times.

someone who brings shame to the family or is the odd one in the family

That vase is a family heirloom. Lou's grandfather bought it in China in 1893.

an object that has been passed down through the generations of a family

We're a close-knit family. We always meet up for birthdays and holidays.

a loyal and supportive family

We're moving to a bigger house because we're hoping to start a family soon.

have children

I am close to my immediate family, but rarely see my other relatives.

close family, such as parents, sons, daughters, brothers, and sisters

We're bringing up our children to be kind to animals.

teaching a child how to behave

Boris often asks members of his extended family to help with childcare.

wider family, such as grandparents, cousins, nephews, and nieces

Curly hair runs in our family, and my daughter, mom, and I all have it.

is a common feature in our family

2.3 MATCH THE DEFINITIONS TO THE CORRECT IDIOMS

	Definition	Idiom
	close family, such as parents, sons, daughters, brothers, and sisters → immediate family	a fair-weather friend
1	an object that has been passed down through the generations of a family	immediate family
2	a friend who deserts you when you have difficulties	losing touch with
3	no longer being in contact with	a family heirloom
4	the perfect person to be a friend or partner	a soulmate
5	slowly become less friendly or close to each other	extended family
6	wider family, such as grandparents, cousins, nephews, and nieces	drifted apart

2.4 LISTEN TO THE AUDIO, THEN NUMBER THE PICTURES IN THE ORDER YOU HEAR THEM

A ☐

B ☐

C 1

D ☐

E ☐

F ☐

G ☐

H ☐

Aa 2.5 CROSS OUT THE INCORRECT WORDS IN EACH SENTENCE

Bob reminds me so much of his father. He is a chip off the old ~~brick~~ / **block** / ~~log~~.

1. We're moving to a bigger house because we're hoping to **begin** / **start** / **have** a family soon.
2. My wife and I **struck** / **hit** / **beat** it off immediately when we first met at a country music concert.
3. Uncle Tony is the black **sheep** / **horse** / **cow** of the family. He's been to prison three times.
4. Cy and I got off on the wrong **hand** / **leg** / **foot** on our date. He was an hour late and forgot my name.
5. Ramón and Tara get on like a **house** / **barn** / **home** on fire. They're always talking and laughing.

Aa 2.6 LOOK AT THE PICTURES AND COMPLETE THE SENTENCES

My wife and I *hit it off* immediately when we first met at a country music concert.

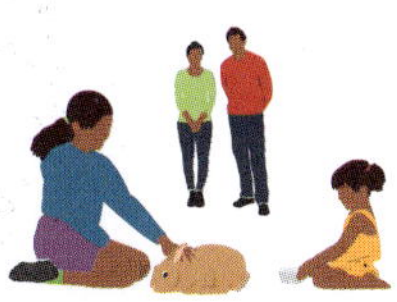

1. We're ______________________ our children to be kind to animals.

2. Marie and Pierre met through Isaac, ______________________ of theirs.

3. Curly hair ______________________, and my daughter, mom, and I all have it.

4. I've ______________________ Lin since we left college 25 years ago.

5. Jade is ______________________. She grew up on the same street as us.

03 Appearance and background

3.1 APPEARANCE

Leo **bears a striking resemblance** to his grandfather.

looks extremely similar

Karen is **the spitting image of** that actor in the new sci-fi film.

almost identical to

Oscar is only 25, but he's already **getting thin on top**. (US)

going bald

Milan returned home with **five o'clock shadow** after a long day at the office.

the beginning of a beard

Edie **looks like butter wouldn't melt in her mouth**, but she's actually really naughty.

looks innocent, like she wouldn't do anything bad

Mateo and his brother Lucas are **like two peas in a pod**. I can't tell them apart.

extremely similar to each other

You must eat something! You're **all skin and bones**.

too thin

Rita **looked like she'd seen a ghost** after I told her my news.

looked very scared or shocked

Rachel **looked like a drowned rat** after she got caught in the rain on her way home.

was very wet

My aunt believed in **keeping up appearances** despite having little money.

pretending that things are going well

3.2 STYLE AND DRESS

Domenica looked the part for her first day of work at the bank.

was dressed in the right way

George arrived at the restaurant immaculately groomed for his date with Cassie.

elegantly dressed and well presented

Clara looked like a million bucks when she arrived for her wedding. (US)

looked extremely glamorous

Nalini never has a hair out of place. She cares a lot about her appearance.

is extremely neat and well groomed

3.3 BACKGROUND, ADVANTAGE, AND DISADVANTAGE

Rebecca has blue blood. Her great-grandmother was a princess.

is descended from important people or aristocracy

Philip was born with a silver spoon in his mouth. He grew up in a castle in France.

was born into a wealthy family

My aunt is a pillar of the community. She supports charities and attends local events.

an important or well-respected person

Maxine is such a highflier. She's been promoted twice this year and is only 23. (US)

a very talented and successful person

Danika's parents don't approve of Bob because he's from the wrong side of the tracks.

the wrong social background or part of town

My parents didn't have two pennies to rub together, but we still had lots of fun.

were very poor

Aa 3.4 READ THE STATEMENTS AND MARK THE CORRECT MEANING

My parents didn't have two pennies to rub together, but we still had lots of fun.
My parents were rich. ☐ **My parents were poor.** ☑

1 My aunt is a pillar of the community. She supports charities and attends local events.
My aunt is a well-respected person. ☐ **My aunt is a dishonest person.** ☐

2 Philip was born with a silver spoon in his mouth. He grew up in a castle in France.
Philip has always been wealthy. ☐ **Philip has always been generous.** ☐

3 Danika's parents don't approve of Bob because he's from the wrong side of the tracks.
Bob is a train driver. ☐ **Bob is from the wrong social background.** ☐

4 Clara looked like a million bucks when she arrived for her wedding.
Clara looked extremely nervous. ☐ **Clara looked extremely glamorous.** ☐

5 Rebecca has blue blood. Her great-grandmother was a princess.
She is descended from important people. ☐ **She is a princess.** ☐

Aa 3.5 REWRITE THE SENTENCES, CORRECTING THE ERRORS

George arrived at the restaurant **immaculately styled** for his date with Cassie.
George arrived at the restaurant immaculately groomed for his date with Cassie.

1 Edie **looks like ice cream wouldn't melt in her mouth**, but she's actually really naughty.

2 Oscar is only 25, but he's already **getting slim on top**.

3 My aunt believed in **holding up appearances** despite having little money.

4 Nalini **never has a hair out of sight**. She cares a lot about her appearance.

5 Milan returned home with **four o'clock shadow** after a long day at the office.

3.6 LISTEN TO THE AUDIO AND COMPLETE THE SENTENCES THAT DESCRIBE EACH PICTURE

Leo *bears a striking resemblance* to his grandfather.

1 Domenica ______________ for her first day of work at the bank.

2 Clara ______________ when she arrived for her wedding.

3 Mateo and his brother Lucas are ______________ . I can't tell them apart.

4 Karen is ______________ that actor in the new sci-fi film.

5 Rita ______________ after I told her my news.

6 Rachel ______________ after she got caught in the rain on her way home.

3.7 WRITE THE CORRECT IDIOM NEXT TO ITS DEFINITION, FILLING IN THE MISSING LETTERS

extremely similar to each other = l *i k e* t *w o* p *e a s* i *n* a p *o d*

1 too thin = a _ _ s _ _ _ a _ _ b _ _ _ _

2 almost identical to = t _ _ s _ _ _ _ _ _ _ i _ _ _ _ o _

3 going bald = g _ _ _ _ _ _ t _ _ _ o _ t _ _

4 the beginning of a beard = f _ _ _ o' _ _ _ _ _ s _ _ _ _ _

5 a very talented and successful person = a h _ _ _ f _ _ _ _

04 Personality traits

4.1 DESCRIBING PERSONALITY

Lucia has a vivid imagination. Her artworks are so original.

an ability to think of exciting images and ideas

Norah is such a fuddy-duddy. She never wants to come out with us on Saturday night.

someone who is unwilling to try new things

Gustav has a selfish streak. He won't share his cookies with his friends.

a tendency to be selfish

Arturo is so two-faced. He said he liked my haircut but told his friends he hated it.

insincere or hypocritical

Chetan is as bold as brass. He walked up to the actor and asked for an autograph.

very confident

My dad's just an average Joe. He enjoys burgers and fries, and loves watching baseball. (US)

a stereotypical man who has simple tastes

It was great to see Jasmine at the party. She's always a barrel of laughs.

a fun person or situation

Bob is such a crybaby. He was very upset about not getting a perfect score.

someone who cries a lot without good reason

Zoe loves proving how much she knows. She's too smart for her own good.

annoyingly proud of her intelligence or knowledge

Noah is really down to earth. He earns lots of money, but he lives in a little cottage.

practical and unpretentious

4.2 IDIOMS USING VOCABULARY ABOUT ANIMALS

I know Rex looks a bit scary, but he wouldn't hurt a fly.

is completely harmless

Claire is a social butterfly. She's always going to parties.

a very sociable person

My uncle's a lone wolf. He lives on his own in a cabin in the forest.

someone who prefers to live or work alone

Tony wouldn't say boo to a goose. He gets really shy when he talks to customers. (UK)

is very timid and nervous

Don't be afraid of Linda. Her bark is worse than her bite.

She's not as scary as she seems.

Ben never told us he could tap dance. He is such a dark horse.

someone who hides a surprising skill or quality

4.3 IDIOMS USING VOCABULARY ABOUT FOOD

Jim's a good egg. He helped me to move last week.

an honest, reliable, or considerate person

Hassan is the salt of the earth. I saw him help an old lady cross the road.

kind, honest, and unpretentious

Debbie's a tough cookie. She doesn't mind when people criticize her work.

determined and physically or emotionally strong

Kirsty remained as cool as a cucumber throughout her performance.

calm and relaxed

4.4 MARK THE SENTENCES THAT ARE CORRECT

Ben never told us he could tap dance. He is such a dark sheep. ☐
Ben never told us he could tap dance. He is such a dark horse. ☑

1 

It was great to see Jasmine at the party. She's always a barrel of laughs. ☐
It was great to see Jasmine at the party. She's always a tub of laughs. ☐

2 

Bob is such a crying baby. He was very upset about not getting a perfect score. ☐
Bob is such a crybaby. He was very upset about not getting a perfect score. ☐

3 

Don't be afraid of Linda. Her bite is worse than her bark. ☐
Don't be afraid of Linda. Her bark is worse than her bite. ☐

4 

Jim's a good egg. He helped me to move last week. ☐
Jim's a good cheese. He helped me to move last week. ☐

5 

Gustav has a selfish streak. He won't share his cookies with his friends. ☐
Gustav has a selfish line. He won't share his cookies with his friends. ☐

6 

Debbie's a tough cake. She doesn't mind when people criticize her work. ☐
Debbie's a tough cookie. She doesn't mind when people criticize her work. ☐

4.5 LISTEN TO THE AUDIO, THEN NUMBER THE SENTENCES IN THE ORDER YOU HEAR THEM

A Lucia has a vivid imagination. Her artworks are so original. ☐

B Chetan is as bold as brass. He walked up to the actor and asked for an autograph. ☐

C My uncle's a lone wolf. He lives on his own in a cabin in the forest. ☐

D Bob is such a crybaby. He was very upset about not getting a perfect score. 1

E I know Rex looks a bit scary, but he wouldn't hurt a fly. ☐

F Zoe loves proving how much she knows. She's too smart for her own good. ☐

G Claire is a social butterfly. She's always going to parties. ☐

H Kirsty remained as cool as a cucumber throughout her performance. ☐

Aa 4.6 MATCH THE PICTURES TO THE CORRECT SENTENCES

1 

2 

3 

4 

5 

My dad's just an average Joe. He enjoys burgers and fries, and he loves watching baseball.

Hassan is the salt of the earth. I saw him help an old lady cross the road.

Noah is really down to earth. He earns lots of money, but he lives in a little cottage.

Arturo is so two-faced. He said he liked my haircut but told his friends he hated it.

Tony wouldn't say boo to a goose. He gets really shy when he talks to customers.

Norah is such a fuddy-duddy. She never wants to come out with us on Saturday night.

Aa 4.7 WRITE THE CORRECT IDIOM NEXT TO ITS DEFINITION

someone who is unwilling to try new things = *a fuddy-duddy*

1 She's not as scary as she seems. = ______

2 calm and relaxed = ______

3 very confident = ______

4 a fun person or situation = ______

5 is completely harmless = ______

05 Good things

5.1 IDIOMS FOR PRAISING THINGS

My kids think this TV show is the best thing since sliced bread.

extremely good

Marcelo stole the show with his amazing singing.

was the best, or attracted the most praise

The ice cream at Giuseppe's parlor really is the bee's knees!

the very best

My new TV is miles ahead of my old one.

much more advanced than

The workmen have done a first-class job on our kitchen. It looks beautiful.

superb

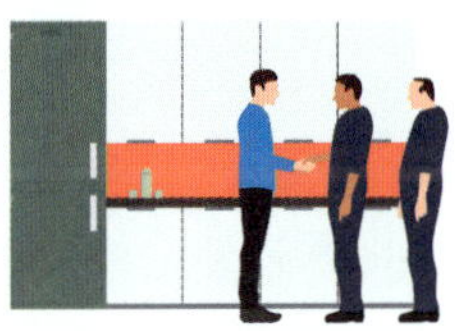

The view from the top of the mountain is totally out of this world. You can see for miles.

amazing

Francisco thinks the world of his grandson. He loves spending time with him.

really likes or admires

World-class athletes need to train for a few hours every day.

among the best in the world

We had a wonderful boat trip. The icing on the cake was seeing some dolphins.

the best part of a good experience

Elisa just moved into the house of her dreams. It's a fabulous lakeside villa.

that she has fantasized about having

Walking to work gives me **the best of both worlds**. It helps me save money and get fit.

the benefits of two different things at the same time

Losing my office job was **a blessing in disguise**. My new job is much more interesting.

something that seems bad, but is actually good

Chan's store only sells watches that are **top of the line**. (US)

the best quality

The burgers in Max's diner are **to die for**. And they're huge!

amazing

The gallery has a **mind-blowing** collection of modern art.

amazing

Laura's play has received **rave reviews**. The critics loved it!

excellent reviews

Javier's performance will be **a tough act to follow**. It was incredible.

difficult to beat

Abel is a **top-notch** reporter. He's interviewed some really famous actors.

highest quality

The crème de la crème of the fashion world were at the launch party.

the very best people

Karolina's cake is **second to none**. It looks beautiful, and it tastes delicious.

far better than any others

5.2 FILL IN THE GAPS, PUTTING THE WORDS IN THE CORRECT ORDER

follow | a | act | tough | to

Javier's performance will be a tough act to follow. It was incredible.

best | sliced | the | thing | bread | since

1 My kids think this TV show is ______ ______ ______ ______ ______ ______.

cake | The | the | icing | on

2 We had a wonderful boat trip. ______ ______ ______ ______ ______ was seeing some dolphins.

line | of | top | the

3 Chan's store only sells watches that are ______ ______ ______ ______.

de | crème | la | The | crème

4 ______ ______ ______ ______ ______ of the fashion world were at the launch party.

5.3 LISTEN TO THE AUDIO, THEN NUMBER THE PICTURES IN THE ORDER YOU HEAR THEM

A ☐

B ☐

C 1

D ☐

E ☐

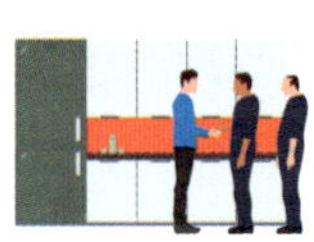

F ☐

5.4 MATCH THE BEGINNINGS OF THE IDIOMS TO THE CORRECT ENDINGS

	top of → the line	of both worlds
1	out of	to none
2	the best	the line
3	second	knees
4	stole the	this world
5	the crème de	in disguise
6	the bee's	la crème
7	a blessing	show

Aa 5.5 MATCH THE IDIOMS TO THE CORRECT DEFINITIONS

	Idiom	Definition
	second to none → far better than any others	excellent reviews
1	top-notch	really likes or admires
2	the icing on the cake	far better than any others
3	rave reviews	that she has fantasized about having
4	thinks the world of	the best part of a good experience
5	of her dreams	highest quality

Aa 5.6 LOOK AT THE PICTURES AND COMPLETE THE SENTENCES

Elisa just moved into the house *of her dreams*. It's a fabulous lakeside villa.

1 ______________________ athletes need to train for a few hours every day.

2 Marcelo ______________________ with his amazing singing.

3 ______________________ of the fashion world were at the launch party.

4 Walking to work gives me ______________________. It helps me save money and get fit.

5 The burgers in Max's diner are ______________________. And they're huge!

06 Bad things

6.1 IDIOMS FOR CRITICIZING THINGS

Pete's habit of dropping litter leaves a bad taste in my mouth.

makes me feel very uncomfortable

The weather in Hawaii didn't live up to expectations. It rained every day.

was not as good as expected

The clothes in this store are second rate. They don't last very long.

low-quality

Country music is not my cup of tea. I prefer rock music.

not something I enjoy

I'm afraid this product just isn't up to scratch, Kyle. (UK)

isn't good enough

Noah's old car is past its prime. He's been driving it for years.

in a bad condition, or too old

I know everyone else loves it, but this book is not all that it's cracked up to be.

not as good as everyone says it is

The museum in my town is nothing to write home about. There are very few exhibits.

not very impressive

The hotel was cheap and nasty. There were cockroaches in my room. (UK)

affordable but low-quality

I was stuck in traffic for three hours on a boiling hot day. It was a fate worse than death!

a very unpleasant experience

Marco's suit **has seen better days**. He should buy a new one.

is in a bad condition

His voice is OK, but he's **not going to set the world on fire**.

not going to be very exciting or successful

It's time you got rid of that **moth-eaten** old sofa of yours.

shabby; in a bad condition

I told my roommate to move out. **The last straw** was when she broke my favorite mug.

the last in a series of events that makes a bad situation impossible to tolerate

Sales **fell short of expectations** last month. We need to do better this month.

were not as good as expected

Watching golf on TV is so boring. It's **like watching paint dry**.

extremely boring

It's still **rough around the edges**, but this is my design for the park.

not perfect; in need of more work

Rita's TV is **on its last legs**. She's had it for over 10 years.

likely to stop working soon

We had been really looking forward to the meal, but thought the food was **a let-down**.

a disappointment

My old desktop computer is **past its sell-by date**. It takes a long time to start up.

in need of replacing

6.2 MATCH THE DEFINITIONS TO THE CORRECT IDIOMS

makes me feel very uncomfortable → leaves a bad taste in my mouth

1. affordable but low-quality
2. extremely boring
3. in need of replacing
4. a very unpleasant experience
5. not something I enjoy
6. not perfect; in need of more work

- past its sell-by date
- like watching paint dry
- leaves a bad taste in my mouth
- cheap and nasty
- rough around the edges
- a fate worse than death
- not my cup of tea

6.3 CROSS OUT THE INCORRECT WORDS IN EACH SENTENCE

Marco's suit has seen better **days** / ~~**times**~~ / ~~**years**~~. He should buy a new one.

1.  The museum in my town is nothing to **write** / **call** / **go** home about. There are very few exhibits.

2.  The weather in Hawaii didn't **get** / **go** / **live** up to expectations. It rained every day.

3.  Rita's TV is on its last **feet** / **legs** / **stand**. She's had it for over 10 years.

4.  The clothes in this store are second **class** / **quality** / **rate**. They don't last very long.

5.  Pete's habit of dropping litter leaves a bad **flavor** / **taste** / **meal** in my mouth.

6.4 LISTEN TO THE AUDIO AND COMPLETE THE SENTENCES THAT DESCRIBE EACH PICTURE

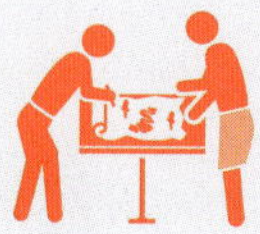

It's still *rough around the edges*, but this is my design for the park.

3 I know everyone else loves it, but this book is ____________________ .

1 I told my roommate to move out. ____________ ____________ was when she broke my favorite mug.

4 I'm afraid this product just ____________ ____________ , Kyle.

2 Sales ____________________ last month. We need to do better this month.

5 His voice is OK, but he's ____________ ____________ .

Aa 6.5 WRITE THE CORRECT IDIOM NEXT TO ITS DEFINITION, FILLING IN THE MISSING LETTERS

not something I enjoy = n *o t* m *y* c *u p* o *f* t *e a*

1 shabby; in a bad condition = m _ _ _ - e _ _ _ _

2 a disappointment = a l _ _ - d _ _ _

3 in a bad condition, or too old = p _ _ _ i _ _ p _ _ _ _

4 low-quality = s _ _ _ _ _ r _ _ _

5 affordable but low-quality = c _ _ _ _ a _ _ n _ _ _ _

07 Animals

7.1 IDIOMS USING VOCABULARY ABOUT ANIMALS

Tim is such a scaredy-cat. He's terrified of spiders.

a person who is very easily scared

I don't think you're really too sick to go to school. You always cry wolf.

pretend there's danger or something wrong when there isn't

Clarita's new apartment is tiny. There's not enough room to swing a cat.

very little space

My colleagues all have terrible colds. They're dropping like flies!

becoming sick, or stopping doing something, in large numbers

You're barking up the wrong tree if you think I can help you with your homework. I'm terrible at science.

wasting effort by following the wrong course of action

Our falling profits are the elephant in the room at every team meeting.

a problem that everyone pretends to ignore

The half-mile run was a two-horse race between Beatriz and Maria.

a competition with only two clear possible winners

I chickened out of diving off the top board in the pool. It was too high!

was too scared to

Flo looked like a deer in headlights when I caught her reading my diary. (US)

too shocked or frightened to move

I told my boss I won't finish my report today, but she still keeps badgering me about it.

repeatedly telling me to do something

Lech is a night owl. He never goes to bed before midnight.

someone who likes to stay up late at night

Bill looked like the cat that got the cream when he won the competition.

very happy, proud, or satisfied

It really gets my goat when someone eats smelly food on the train.

irritates me

We had a bird's-eye view of the city from the hot-air balloon.

a long-distance view from above

Rachel always gets on her high horse about being a vegetarian. It's so annoying!

adopts a morally superior attitude

You can do anything now that you've finished college. The world is your oyster.

You have lots of opportunities.

Frank ate the lion's share of the cake. There wasn't enough for us!

the largest part

Ruby is a one-trick pony. She's a great singer, but she can't dance or act.

someone with only one talent or skill

I tried to fix the photocopier, but I've really made a pig's ear of it. (UK)

done it very badly

Jenny didn't mind when her friends laughed at her coat. It was water off a duck's back.

not at all upsetting

7.2 LISTEN TO THE AUDIO, THEN NUMBER THE SENTENCES IN THE ORDER YOU HEAR THEM

A I don't think you're really too sick to go to school. You always cry wolf. ☐

B Lech is a night owl. He never goes to bed before midnight. ☐

C Frank ate the lion's share of the cake. There wasn't enough for us! ☐

D Jenny didn't mind when her friends laughed at her coat. It was water off a duck's back. ☐

E I told my boss I won't finish my report today, but she still keeps badgering me about it. 1

F The half-mile run was a two-horse race between Beatriz and Maria. ☐

7.3 MATCH THE PICTURES TO THE CORRECT SENTENCES

1 

2 

3 

4 

5 

You're barking up the wrong tree if you think I can help you with your homework. I'm terrible at science.

Jenny didn't mind when her friends laughed at her coat. It was water off a duck's back.

It really gets my goat when someone eats smelly food on the train.

Our falling profits are the elephant in the room at every team meeting.

Rachel always gets on her high horse about being a vegetarian. It's so annoying!

Bill looked like the cat that got the cream when he won the competition.

Aa 7.4 CROSS OUT THE INCORRECT WORDS IN EACH SENTENCE

Frank ate the **lion's** / ~~**tiger's**~~ / ~~**bear's**~~ share of the cake. There wasn't enough for us!

1 I tried to fix the photocopier, but I've really made a **cow's** / **sheep's** / **pig's** ear of it.

2 My colleagues all have terrible colds. They're **dropping** / **falling** / **buzzing** like flies!

3 Ruby is a one-trick **horse** / **pony** / **donkey**. She's a great singer, but she can't dance or act.

4 I **pigged** / **chickened** / **cowed** out of diving off the top board in the pool. It was too high!

5 Clarita's new apartment is tiny. There's not enough room to swing a **mouse** / **frog** / **cat**.

Aa 7.5 WRITE THE CORRECT IDIOM NEXT TO ITS DEFINITION

someone with only one talent or skill = *a one-trick pony*

1 irritates me = ______

2 very little space = ______

3 a long-distance view from above = ______

4 a person who is very easily scared = ______

5 You have lots of opportunities. = ______

6 too shocked or frightened to move = ______

08 Food

8.1 IDIOMS USING VOCABULARY ABOUT FOOD AND DRINK

We thought our walk would be really hilly, but the land was **as flat as a pancake.**

very flat

I don't like my job, but it **puts food on the table.**

provides enough money to pay for the most important things

We're usually **packed like sardines** on the bus to work in the morning.

standing very close to each other

Sharon always **spoon-feeds** her staff. She tells them exactly what to do.

gives too much help to

Our boss tried to **sugarcoat** the news that we wouldn't get a bonus by saying we'd have a summer party.

make something bad sound better than it is

Don't get so upset about burning the cookies. It's no use **crying over spilled milk.**

getting upset about something that has already happened

Jennifer is such **a couch potato.** She never goes out and watches TV all weekend instead.

a lazy person who watches too much television

Damien makes coffee for his boss every morning. He **knows what side his bread is buttered on!**

knows who to please in order to benefit himself

My granddaughter is **the apple of my eye.** I'm so proud of her.

a person I am very fond or proud of

I don't know whether to apply for this job. It looks really interesting, but **it pays peanuts.**

the wage or salary is very low

I bought so many clothes that I can't afford a vacation. I suppose you can't have your cake and eat it, too.

you can't enjoy the benefits of something without its disadvantages

I know Aiden's always late, but arriving late for his own wedding takes the cake! (US)

is particularly bad

I felt warm and toasty sitting in front of the fire. (US)

very warm and comfortable

Asher is such a butterfingers. He is always dropping things.

a clumsy person who often drops things

The head of sales said he would double our profits, so he had to eat humble pie when he told us they had fallen.

publicly admit to being wrong or having failed

Fiona told me she doesn't like my new scooter. I think it's just sour grapes.

a jealous and bitter attitude

I'm really stressed! I think I bit off more than I could chew when I took this promotion.

took on more responsibility than I could manage

I wanted Jo to water my plants when I was on vacation, so I buttered her up by saying her backyard looked nice.

praised or flattered her so she would do me a favor

Copies of Sadie's new novel are selling like hotcakes after it got great reviews.

selling quickly in large numbers

You have to walk on eggshells around Dylan. He gets upset so easily.

be very careful not to cause offense

Aa 8.2 MATCH THE BEGINNINGS OF THE STATEMENTS TO THE CORRECT ENDINGS

Sharon always spoon-feeds her staff. → She tells them exactly what to do.

1. We're usually packed like sardines
2. My granddaughter is the apple of my eye.
3. We thought our walk would be really hilly,
4. I felt warm and toasty
5. I don't like my job,
6. You have to walk on eggshells around Dylan.

- on the bus to work in the morning.
- but the land was as flat as a pancake.
- She tells them exactly what to do.
- He gets upset so easily.
- I'm so proud of her.
- sitting in front of the fire.
- but it puts food on the table.

Aa 8.3 MARK THE SENTENCES THAT ARE CORRECT

Don't get so upset about burning the cookies. It's no use crying over spilled water. ☐
Don't get so upset about burning the cookies. It's no use crying over spilled milk. ☑

1 

I know Aiden's always late, but arriving late for his own wedding takes the bread! ☐
I know Aiden's always late, but arriving late for his own wedding takes the cake! ☐

2 

I'm really stressed! I think I bit off more than I could chew when I took this promotion. ☐
I'm really stressed! I think I bit off more than I could eat when I took this promotion. ☐

3 

Fiona told me she doesn't like my new scooter. I think it's just sour grapes. ☐
Fiona told me she doesn't like my new scooter. I think it's just bitter grapes. ☐

4 

Asher is such a butterhands. He is always dropping things. ☐
Asher is such a butterfingers. He is always dropping things. ☐

5 

Copies of Sadie's new novel are selling like hotbuns after it got great reviews. ☐
Copies of Sadie's new novel are selling like hotcakes after it got great reviews. ☐

8.4 LISTEN TO THE AUDIO AND MARK THE CORRECT PICTURE FOR EACH SENTENCE YOU HEAR

A ☑ B ☐ C ☐

1

A ☐ B ☐ C ☐

2

A ☐ B ☐ C ☐

3

A ☐ B ☐ C ☐

4

A ☐ B ☐ C ☐

5

A ☐ B ☐ C ☐

8.5 WRITE THE CORRECT IDIOM NEXT TO ITS DEFINITION

took on more responsibility than I could manage = *bit off more than I could chew*

1. publicly admit to being wrong or having failed = ______
2. a lazy person who watches too much television = ______
3. gives too much help to = ______
4. be very careful not to cause offense = ______
5. make something bad sound better than it is = ______

09 Agreeing and disagreeing

9.1 AGREEMENT AND UNDERSTANDING

We're on the same page about who should get this job.

in agreement

Samira has been given the go-ahead to play tennis after her injury.

given permission or approval

It's great to work with the creative people in this team. We're all on the same wavelength.

similar in terms of thoughts, ideas, or attitude

The government has given the green light to the construction of a new train station.

given permission for

Fran's dad gave her the thumbs-up to go out with her friends.

gave her permission

I'm glad my boss and I see eye to eye about recycling in the office.

agree fully or have a similar attitude

9.3 COMPROMISE

We struck a deal with the clients after we offered them a discount.

reached an agreement

We found the middle ground about how much to spend on our new car.

a position between two different opinions, or a compromise

Diana and I reached a compromise about what movie to watch tonight.

came to an agreement

My son wanted to stay out all night. I met him halfway and let him stay out until midnight.

made a compromise

9.2 DISAGREEMENT AND CONFLICT

Nelson and Carole are **at odds** about which car to buy.

unable to agree

Don **jumped down my throat** when I suggested he clean the kitchen.

reacted angrily

My girlfriend and I have **agreed to disagree** about what to do on vacation.

accepted each other's differing opinion

Who takes the dog for a walk is **a bone of contention** for our kids.

a subject that people argue about regularly

My wife **read me the riot act** for forgetting to lock the door again.

severely reprimanded me

Lenka and I **fought like cats and dogs** when we were children.

argued all the time

The negotiating teams stayed up all night **hammering out a deal**.

reaching an agreement after a long discussion

My neighbor and I have **buried the hatchet** after arguing about the parking.

ended an argument that has lasted a long time

I tried to **smooth things over** between Pari and Toni after their argument.

make a problem or conflict feel less serious

After arguing with Dan, Cy **held out an olive branch** and bought him a drink.

did something to end a conflict

Aa 9.4 REWRITE THE SENTENCES, CORRECTING THE ERRORS

I'm glad my boss and I **see face to face** about recycling in the office.
I'm glad my boss and I see eye to eye about recycling in the office.

1. My neighbor and I have **buried the ax** after arguing about the parking.

2. The negotiating teams stayed up all night **drilling out a deal**.

3. The government has **given the red light to** the construction of a new train station.

4. My girlfriend and I have **agreed to change** about what to do on vacation.

9.5 LISTEN TO THE AUDIO, THEN NUMBER THE PICTURES IN THE ORDER YOU HEAR THEM

A ☐

B 1

C ☐

D ☐

E ☐

F ☐

G ☐

H ☐

I ☐

Aa 9.6 READ THE LETTER AND CROSS OUT THE INCORRECT WORDS

Hi Fiona,
How are you? I had some problems at work recently. My boss and I are usually on the same page / ~~sheet~~ about work, but we were at offs / odds about my hours. She jumped down my mouth / throat when I said I couldn't work this weekend. We found the middle / central ground when I agreed to stay late on Friday.
See you soon,
Pablo

Aa 9.7 MATCH THE PICTURES TO THE CORRECT SENTENCES

Fran's dad gave her the thumbs-up to go out with her friends.

My son wanted to stay out all night. I met him halfway and let him stay out until midnight.

1 

Lenka and I fought like cats and dogs when we were children.

2 

Diana and I reached a compromise about what movie to watch tonight.

3 

Samira has been given the go-ahead to play tennis after her injury.

4 

I tried to smooth things over between Pari and Toni after their argument.

5 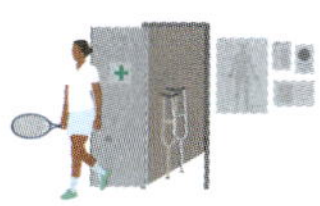

Aa 9.8 WRITE THE CORRECT IDIOM NEXT TO ITS DEFINITION, FILLING IN THE MISSING LETTERS

reacted angrily = jumped down my throat

1. did something to end a conflict = h _ _ _ o _ _ a _ o _ _ _ _ b _ _ _ _ _
2. in agreement = o _ t _ _ s _ _ _ p _ _ _
3. unable to agree = a _ o _ _ _
4. reached an agreement = s _ _ _ _ _ a d _ _ _
5. gave her permission = g _ _ _ h _ _ t _ _ t _ _ _ _ _ - u _

10 Behavior

10.1 SYMPATHY AND KINDNESS

Yulia offered to lend a hand with the dishes after the party.

help

I really feel for Mario. He has to work so hard in the kitchen.

sympathize with

Semir is generous to a fault. He invited us into his home for a wonderful meal.

extremely generous

Yoshiko offered a sympathetic ear when my cat went missing.

offered to listen to someone's problems

Alex is so big hearted. She bought me a beautiful vase for my new apartment.

kind and generous

10.2 TREATING PEOPLE BADLY

Pedro quit his job at the store, leaving me in the lurch.

leaving me to deal with a difficult situation

Phil gave me a hard time about being late for work again.

made me feel guilty, or told me off

The boss makes the trainees stay until 11 most nights. She treats them like dirt!

treats them very badly

Laughing at Sandy's new dress was below the belt.

unnecessarily cruel or unkind

Selma let us down when she canceled the concert at the last minute.

disappointed us, or failed to support us

10.3 TEASING PEOPLE

Paulina poked fun at Mirek's new hairstyle.

laughed at or made jokes about

My friends ribbed me for having such an old phone. (US)

teased me

Aziz told me he'd crashed my car, but he was pulling my leg.

joking, or telling an untrue story for fun

Brad loves playing practical jokes on his brother.

playing tricks on people to make them look foolish

10.4 EXPRESSIONS WITH "BEHAVE" AND "BEHAVIOR"

The children were very well behaved during the performance.

polite or obedient

My dog behaved beautifully when I took him on the train.

behaved perfectly

Henry can't control his badly behaved students.

naughty or disobedient

I was on my best behavior when I met my boyfriend's parents.

behaving extremely well or politely

Jean behaved out of character at the office party. She's normally so quiet!

behaved in an unusual way

Margo explained to her daughter that drawing on the walls was unacceptable behavior.

bad or offensive behavior

10.5 MARK THE SENTENCES THAT ARE CORRECT

Phil gave me a hard time about being late for work again. ☑
Phil gave me a nasty time about being late for work again. ☐

1 

Yoshiko offered a sympathetic listen when my cat went missing. ☐
Yoshiko offered a sympathetic ear when my cat went missing. ☐

2 

Aziz told me he'd crashed my car, but he was pulling my leg. ☐
Aziz told me he'd crashed my car, but he was pulling my arm. ☐

3 

I was on my best behavior when I met my boyfriend's parents. ☐
I was on my good behavior when I met my boyfriend's parents. ☐

4 

Pedro quit his job at the store, leaving me in the dumps. ☐
Pedro quit his job at the store, leaving me in the lurch. ☐

5 

Jean behaved out of character at the office party. She's normally so quiet! ☐
Jean behaved out of person at the office party. She's normally so quiet! ☐

6 

Paulina poked laughs at Mirek's new hairstyle. ☐
Paulina poked fun at Mirek's new hairstyle. ☐

10.6 WRITE THE IDIOMS FROM THE PANEL IN THE CORRECT GROUPS

GOOD BEHAVIOR	BAD BEHAVIOR
generous to a fault	

below the belt · ~~generous to a fault~~ · big hearted · treats them like dirt · behaved beautifully · let us down · unacceptable behavior · lend a hand

10.7 LISTEN TO THE AUDIO, THEN NUMBER THE SENTENCES IN THE ORDER YOU HEAR THEM

A The children were very well behaved during the performance. ☐

B Laughing at Sandy's new dress was below the belt. ☐

C Selma let us down when she canceled the concert at the last minute. ☐

D Margo explained to her daughter that drawing on the walls was unacceptable behavior. [1]

E Yulia offered to lend a hand with the dishes after the party. ☐

10.8 LOOK AT THE PICTURES AND COMPLETE THE SENTENCES

Laughing at Sandy's new dress was *below the belt*.

3 My friends ______________________ for having such an old phone.

1 Henry can't control his ______________________ students.

4 My dog ______________________ when I took him on the train.

2 I really ______________________ Mario. He has to work so hard in the kitchen.

5 Brad loves ______________________ on his brother.

11 Emotions

11.1 IDIOMS USING VOCABULARY ABOUT THE BODY

They can't stop arguing. They're always at each other's throats.

very aggressive and argumentative with each other

You can always tell when he's upset. He wears his heart on his sleeve.

makes his feelings obvious

Caitlin got cold feet about singing karaoke.

became too nervous to do something

Leo cried his eyes out when I said he couldn't have another cookie.

cried uncontrollably

It was a weight off my shoulders when Mark found my cat. She had been missing for a week.

a huge relief

People in my town are up in arms about plans to build a new supermarket.

very angry, or protesting against something

11.2 IDIOMS USING VOCABULARY ABOUT COLORS

Liz was feeling blue when her best friend left the country.

feeling sad

My neighbor saw red when I parked in front of his house.

became angry

I was green with envy when Jamila showed me her new house. It was so big!

very jealous

Silvio went as white as a sheet when he got the bad news.

very pale because of shock or fear

When Dylan copied her homework, Zoe was so angry that she was foaming at the mouth.

extremely angry

After a long week at work, I let my hair down at my best friend's party.

relaxed and enjoyed myself

I was broken-hearted when my girlfriend left me.

very upset, usually after the end of a romantic relationship

I get itchy feet when I haven't been abroad for a long time.

boredom with being in the same place or situation

I became tongue-tied when I had to give a presentation to the board of directors.

too nervous to speak

I was really upset when a customer shouted at me, but I managed to keep a stiff upper lip.

appear calm despite being upset

11.3 IDIOMS USING VOCABULARY ABOUT FOOD

The children all went bananas when I took them to the playground.

were out of control with excitement

This terrible weather is driving me nuts.

annoying me

Akio was full of beans when he started his new job at the salon.

very excited and enthusiastic

I had egg on my face after I called Jo's new boyfriend Ben. That was her ex-boyfriend's name!

was embarrassed

Aa 11.4 REWRITE THE SENTENCES, CORRECTING THE ERRORS

I was **yellow with envy** when Jamila showed me her new house. It was so big!

I was green with envy when Jamila showed me her new house. It was so big!

1 I get **itchy legs** when I haven't been abroad for a long time.

____

2 Liz was **feeling green** when her best friend left the country.

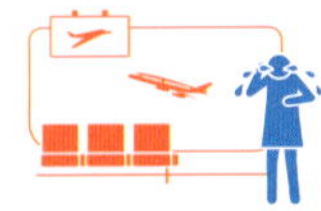

____

3 When Dylan copied her homework, Zoe was so angry that she was **foaming at the lips**.

____

4 This terrible weather is **driving me fruit**.

____

5 My neighbor **saw purple** when I parked in front of his house.

____

11.5 LISTEN TO THE AUDIO, THEN NUMBER THE SENTENCES IN THE ORDER YOU HEAR THEM

A I became tongue-tied when I had to give a presentation to the board of directors. ☐

B They can't stop arguing. They're always at each other's throats. *1*

C It was a weight off my shoulders when Mark found my cat. She had been missing for a week. ☐

D I was green with envy when Jamila showed me her new house. It was so big! ☐

E The children all went bananas when I took them to the playground. ☐

F Leo cried his eyes out when I said he couldn't have another cookie. ☐

G You can always tell when he's upset. He wears his heart on his sleeve. ☐

H Akio was full of beans when he started his new job at the salon. ☐

Aa 11.6 MATCH THE BEGINNINGS OF THE SENTENCES TO THE CORRECT ENDINGS

People in my town are up in arms → about plans to build a new supermarket.

1. I was broken-hearted
2. I get itchy feet when I haven't
3. Caitlin got cold feet
4. The children all went bananas
5. My neighbor saw red

- when my girlfriend left me.
- been abroad for a long time.
- about plans to build a new supermarket.
- when I parked in front of his house.
- about singing karaoke.
- when I took them to the playground.

Aa 11.7 LOOK AT THE PICTURES AND COMPLETE THE SENTENCES

It was *a weight off my shoulders* when Mark found my cat. She had been missing for a week.

3. Silvio went ______________________ when he got the bad news.

1. I ______________________ after I called Jo's new boyfriend Ben. That was her ex-boyfriend's name!

4. I was really upset when a customer shouted at me, but I managed to ______________________ .

2. After a long week at work, I ______________________ ______________ at my best friend's party.

5. Leo ______________________ when I said he couldn't have another cookie.

12 Positive emotions

12.1 HAPPINESS

Clare was on cloud nine after she was promoted.

delighted, extremely happy

Jack was on top of the world when his team won the trophy.

delighted, extremely happy

Dan grinned from ear to ear when he read his test results.

smiled with extreme happiness

The news that our profits were up was music to our ears.

wonderful news

I was over the moon when I won the best actor award.

delighted, extremely happy

Anne is head over heels with that boy she met at the festival.

very much in love

12.2 EXPRESSIONS WITH "JOY"

My motorcycle is my pride and joy. I clean it every day.

something that makes me happy and is important to me

The kids jumped for joy when I brought our new puppy home.

were extremely happy

Brendan wept with joy when he won the talent competition.

cried with happiness

The sight of the park in spring is a joy to behold.

wonderful to look at

12.3 ENTHUSIASM

Two minutes before the race, the athletes were all raring to go.

eager to start doing something

Salvador loves cooking. He puts his heart and soul into it.

puts a lot of effort and enthusiasm into

Our new intern is such an eager beaver. She works really hard.

an enthusiastic person

Robbie has flung himself into training for the gymnastics competition.

done something with lots of enthusiasm and energy

Clara was bright-eyed and bushy-tailed as she set off on the hike.

full of enthusiasm and energy

12.4 EXCITEMENT

I was on the edge of my seat as the detective revealed the murderer.

waiting with nervous excitement

We waited with bated breath for the judge to announce the winner.

with both anxiety and enthusiasm

The children were bouncing off the walls after a whole day indoors.

too excited and full of energy

Sally was bursting with excitement as her favorite band came on stage.

extremely excited

Jamal had butterflies in his stomach as he waited for his date outside the restaurant.

was excited and nervous

Aa 12.5 CROSS OUT THE INCORRECT WORDS IN EACH SENTENCE

Jack was on top of the ~~earth~~ / **world** / ~~planet~~ when his team won the trophy.

1. The news that our profits were up was **singing** / **noise** / **music** to our ears.
2. Our new intern is such an **eager** / **enthusiastic** / **able** beaver. She works really hard.
3. I was over the **moon** / **world** / **stars** when I won the best actor award.
4. Salvador loves cooking. He puts his **mind** / **heart** / **strength** and soul into it.
5. I was on the edge of my **chair** / **stool** / **seat** as the detective revealed the murderer.

12.6 LISTEN TO THE AUDIO AND COMPLETE THE SENTENCES THAT DESCRIBE EACH PICTURE

We waited *with bated breath* for the judge to announce the winner.

1. The kids ______________________ when I brought our new puppy home.

2. Robbie has ______________________ training for the gymnastics competition.

3. My motorcycle is ______________________. I clean it every day.

4. Jamal ______________________ as he waited for his date outside the restaurant.

5. Clara was ______________________ as she set off on the hike.

Aa 12.7 FILL IN THE GAPS, PUTTING THE WORDS IN THE CORRECT ORDER

ear | ear | from | grinned | to

Dan *grinned* *from* *ear* *to* *ear* when he read his test results.

the | off | walls | bouncing

1 The children were ______ ______ ______ ______ after a whole day indoors.

ears | to | music | our

2 The news that our profits were up was ______ ______ ______ ______ .

world | of | on | the | top

3 Jack was ______ ______ ______ ______ ______ when his team won the trophy.

the | my | edge | seat | on | of

4 I was ______ ______ ______ ______ ______ ______ as the detective revealed the murderer.

a | behold | joy | to

5 The sight of the park in spring is ______ ______ ______ ______ .

Aa 12.8 WRITE THE CORRECT IDIOM NEXT TO ITS DEFINITION, FILLING IN THE MISSING LETTERS

too excited and full of energy = b *o u n c i n g* o *f f* t *h e* w *a l l s*

1 extremely excited = b _ _ _ _ _ _ _ w _ _ _ e _ _ _ _ _ _ _ _ _

2 delighted, extremely happy = o _ c _ _ _ _ n _ _ _

3 very much in love = h _ _ _ o _ _ _ h _ _ _ _

4 cried with happiness = w _ _ _ w _ _ _ j _ _

5 eager to start doing something = r _ _ _ _ _ t _ g _

13 Negative emotions

13.1 SADNESS

Joseph has been down in the dumps since his girlfriend left him.

feeling sad

Yannis had a lump in his throat when he said goodbye to his son.

felt like he was going to cry

It was with a heavy heart that I decided to leave my job at the gallery.

with sadness

Carlos was reduced to tears when Marta was mean about his cooking.

upset enough to cry

I've taken you for a day out at the beach. Why are you being such a downer? (US)

a grumpy and disagreeable person

13.2 ANGER

It makes my blood boil when people litter.

makes me really angry

Jason's loud music is really driving me crazy.

annoying me

I kicked myself when I realized I had left my bag on the train.

was angry with myself

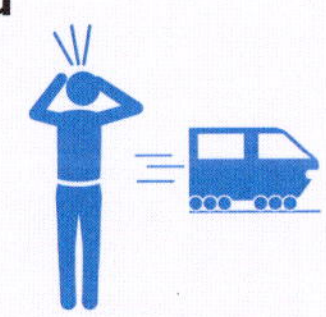

Dad hit the roof when he heard I'd failed my tests again.

quickly became extremely angry

Our boss is on the warpath about people leaving their computers on overnight.

angry and ready for conflict

13.3 FEAR

Jen got that sinking feeling when she realized she had lost her keys.

the feeling that something bad is going to happen

That horror movie sent shivers down my spine. It was so scary!

made me feel very frightened

My blood ran cold when I heard a strange noise outside.

I suddenly felt very afraid

Christine felt on edge as she waited to see her dentist.

nervous or anxious

The sight of the old, spooky house made my hair stand on end.

made me terrified

Alice was shaking in her boots before she did her first bungee jump. (US)

very frightened and nervous

13.4 EMBARRASSMENT

Stella lost face when she got the figures wrong in her presentation.

lost respect, or felt embarrassed

Nina wanted the earth to swallow her up when her dad showed her boyfriend pictures of her as a baby.

wanted to escape an embarrassing situation

I almost died of shame when my girlfriend found me singing in front of the mirror.

was extremely embarrassed

The players left the field with their tails between their legs after losing the game.

looking embarrassed or ashamed

Aa 13.5 READ THE STATEMENTS AND MARK THE CORRECT MEANING

Dad hit the roof when he heard I'd failed my tests again.

Dad was happy. ☐
Dad was angry. ☑
Dad was excited. ☐

1 Yannis had a lump in his throat when he said goodbye to his son.

Yannis was sad. ☐
Yannis was angry. ☐
Yannis was afraid. ☐

2 I almost died of shame when my girlfriend found me singing in front of the mirror.

I was sad. ☐
I was angry. ☐
I was embarrassed. ☐

3 It was with a heavy heart that I decided to leave my job at the gallery.

I was sad. ☐
I was angry. ☐
I was afraid. ☐

4 My blood ran cold when I heard a strange noise outside.

I was angry. ☐
I was afraid. ☐
I was embarrassed. ☐

5 The players left the field with their tails between their legs after losing the game.

They were afraid. ☐
They were angry. ☐
They were ashamed. ☐

13.6 LISTEN TO THE AUDIO AND MARK THE CORRECT PICTURE FOR EACH SENTENCE YOU HEAR

A ☑ B ☐ C ☐

1

A ☐ B ☐ C ☐

2

A ☐ B ☐ C ☐

3

A ☐ B ☐ C ☐

4

A ☐ B ☐ C ☐

5

A ☐ B ☐ C ☐

Aa 13.7 MATCH THE PICTURES TO THE CORRECT SENTENCES

1 

2 

3 

4 

- The sight of the old, spooky house made my hair stand on end.
- I almost died of shame when my girlfriend found me singing in front of the mirror.
- It makes my blood boil when people litter.
- That horror movie sent shivers down my spine. It was so scary!
- Alice was shaking in her boots before she did her first bungee jump.

Aa 13.8 WRITE THE CORRECT IDIOM NEXT TO ITS DEFINITION

made me terrified = *made my hair stand on end*

1 a grumpy and disagreeable person = ____________________

2 angry and ready for conflict = ____________________

3 upset enough to cry = ____________________

4 the feeling that something bad is going to happen = ____________________

5 wanted to escape an embarrassing situation = ____________________

6 was angry with myself = ____________________

14 Memory

14.1 IDIOMS AND EXPRESSIONS ABOUT MEMORY

The answer to the teacher's question was on the tip of my tongue.

almost but not quite remembered

I can't believe I forgot to bring the sandwiches! I've got a memory like a sieve.

a poor practical memory

That boring lecture went in one ear and out the other!

was very easy to forget

Memories are fading of what the world was like before TV.

most people have forgotten

You should keep in mind that it gets cold in the winter and pack some warm clothes. (US)

remember something important that might be useful later

Jacob was explaining the diagram when he suddenly lost his train of thought.

forgot the main point of what he was talking about

When my son asked me to recommend a book, two titles sprang to mind immediately.

came quickly into someone's mind

Martha has a photographic memory. She copied that painting perfectly and she'd only seen it once.

the ability to remember information or images in great detail

It's the worst winter in living memory. I've never seen so much snow.

that anyone alive can remember

The police showed me a photo of the suspect to jog my memory.

help me to remember

When the hotel receptionist asked me for my phone number, **my mind went blank**.

I couldn't remember anything at all

I'm sorry I didn't get you a present. **It slipped my mind** that it was your birthday.

I forgot

That name **rings a bell**! I think I went to college with her.

is familiar

I've seen that animal before, but **its name escapes me**.

I can't remember its name

I've been **racking my brain** all morning but can't remember where I put my passport. (US)

thinking hard, or making an effort to remember

I enjoyed the party, but **at the back of my mind** I knew I had to catch the last train home.

although I tried not to think about it

When Betty found her old teddy bear, **memories** of her childhood **came flooding back**.

memories suddenly returned

Looking at my old medals **stirred up memories** of competing in the Olympics.

brought back memories

Emi and Sofia **took a trip down memory lane** as they talked about their school days.

talked about the past in a happy way

Keeping busy at work is helping me **erase the memory of** my ex-girlfriend.

avoid remembering or thinking about

Aa 14.2 FILL IN THE GAPS, PUTTING THE WORDS IN THE CORRECT ORDER

tip | on | of | tongue | the | my

The answer to the teacher's question was *on the tip of my tongue*.

went | one | and | out | the | ear | other | in

1 That boring lecture ________ ________ ________ ________ ________ ________ ________ ________!

me | name | its | escapes

2 I've seen that animal before, but ________ ________ ________ ________.

memory | trip | a | lane | took | down

3 Emi and Sofia ________ ________ ________ ________ ________ ________ as they talked about their school days.

train | his | thought | lost | of

4 Jacob was explaining the diagram when he suddenly ________ ________ ________ ________ ________.

Aa 14.3 CROSS OUT THE INCORRECT WORD IN EACH SENTENCE

It's the worst winter in living ~~mind~~ / **memory**. I've never seen so much snow.

1  You should keep in **mind** / **memory** that it gets cold in the winter and pack some warm clothes.

2  The police showed me a photo of the suspect to jog my **mind** / **memory**.

3  I enjoyed the party, but at the back of my **mind** / **memory** I knew I had to catch the last train home.

4  Keeping busy at work is helping me erase the **mind** / **memory** of my ex-girlfriend.

14.4 LISTEN TO THE AUDIO AND COMPLETE THE SENTENCES THAT DESCRIBE EACH PICTURE

Looking at my old medals *stirred up memories* of competing in the Olympics.

1 When the hotel receptionist asked me for my phone number, ____________________ .

2 The answer to the teacher's question was ____________________ .

3 I'm sorry I didn't get you a present. ____________________ that it was your birthday.

4 I can't believe I forgot to bring the sandwiches! I've got ____________________ .

5 ____________________ of what the world was like before TV.

14.5 WRITE THE CORRECT IDIOM NEXT TO ITS DEFINITION

I can't remember its name = *its name escapes me*

1 the ability to remember information or images in great detail = ____________________

2 memories suddenly returned = ____________________

3 thinking hard, or making an effort to remember = ____________________

4 is familiar = ____________________

5 avoid remembering or thinking about = ____________________

6 brought back memories = ____________________

7 that anyone alive can remember = ____________________

8 came quickly into someone's mind = ____________________

15 The body

15.1 IDIOMS USING VOCABULARY ABOUT THE BODY

Harjit **has his heart set on** getting a pet.

wants to get or achieve something very much

Maureen was **a bundle of nerves** before her wedding.

extremely nervous

When you're a parent, you need to **have eyes in the back of your head**!

know everything that's going on around you

Scarlett **got cold feet** about going on the rollercoaster.

became too nervous to do something

As **a rule of thumb**, it takes about 10 minutes to cook pasta.

a general, approximate rule based on experience

Boris deserves **a pat on the back** for making this beautiful table.

a lot of appreciation

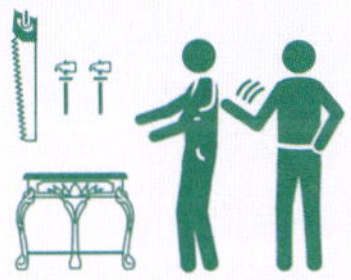

Keep your chin up! I'm sure the weather will get better soon.

Try to stay cheerful, even if circumstances are difficult.

Wyatt is a good friend. He was **a shoulder to cry on** when I broke up with my girlfriend.

a sympathetic and supportive person

I haven't booked a restaurant for lunch, so let's **play it by ear** and find somewhere that looks nice.

do something without planning ahead

You've been to Bali, haven't you? Can I **pick your brain** about the best places to visit?

ask for your opinion and advice

Paolo **almost jumped out of his skin** when a bat flew into his room.

was very shocked or frightened

I can't believe Iris is starting school today. She has grown up **in the blink of an eye**.

very quickly

Oh, no! I've forgotten my wallet. I'm such **a scatterbrain**!

a careless person who forgets things easily

Isla has such **a sweet tooth**. She loves eating cakes.

a liking for sweet food

I hope the performance goes well, Adam. **Break a leg!**

Good luck! (said before performing on stage)

I wish Nathan would turn his music down. It's **getting on my nerves**.

annoying me

There's nothing to do at work at the moment. I'm just sitting here **twiddling my thumbs**.

doing nothing

My heart sank when I got to the museum and saw that it was closed.

I felt sad and disappointed

Our profits keep falling, but our boss is **burying his head in the sand** and not doing anything about it.

ignoring a problem and hoping it will go away

You have to be very **thick-skinned** when you work in this job. The customers often get angry.

not easily upset by criticism

15.2 MATCH THE BEGINNINGS OF THE IDIOMS TO THE CORRECT ENDINGS

	a rule	of nerves
1	burying his head	my nerves
2	a bundle	of thumb
3	getting on	in the sand
4	Keep your	on the back
5	a shoulder	set on
6	a pat	chin up!
7	has his heart	to cry on

(Example: a rule → of thumb)

15.3 LISTEN TO THE AUDIO, THEN NUMBER THE PICTURES IN THE ORDER YOU HEAR THEM

A ☐

B ☐

C ☐

D 1

E ☐

F ☐

G ☐

H ☐

I ☐

15.4 MARK THE SENTENCES THAT ARE CORRECT

Keep your chin up! I'm sure the weather will get better soon. ☑
Keep your head up! I'm sure the weather will get better soon. ☐

1. I hope the performance goes well, Adam. Break a leg! ☐
   I hope the performance goes well, Adam. Break a bone! ☐

2. Oh, no! I've forgotten my wallet. I'm such a scatterhead! ☐
   Oh, no! I've forgotten my wallet. I'm such a scatterbrain! ☐

3. Isla has such a sweet tongue. She loves eating cakes. ☐
   Isla has such a sweet tooth. She loves eating cakes. ☐

4. Wyatt is a good friend. He was a shoulder to cry on when I broke up with my girlfriend. ☐
   Wyatt is a good friend. He was an arm to cry on when I broke up with my girlfriend. ☐

Aa 15.5 MATCH THE DEFINITIONS TO THE CORRECT IDIOMS

	ask for your opinion and advice → pick your brain	play it by ear
1	do something without planning ahead	my heart sank
2	I felt sad and disappointed	pick your brain
3	was very shocked or frightened	has his heart set on
4	wants to get or achieve something very much	thick-skinned
5	not easily upset by criticism	almost jumped out of his skin

Aa 15.6 LOOK AT THE PICTURES AND COMPLETE THE SENTENCES

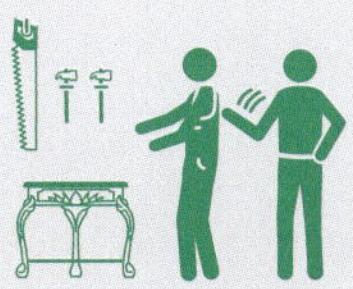

Boris deserves *a pat on the back* for making this beautiful table.

3 Scarlett ______________________ about going on the rollercoaster.

1 Oh, no! I've forgotten my wallet. I'm such ______________________ !

4 There's nothing to do at work at the moment. I'm just sitting here ______________________ .

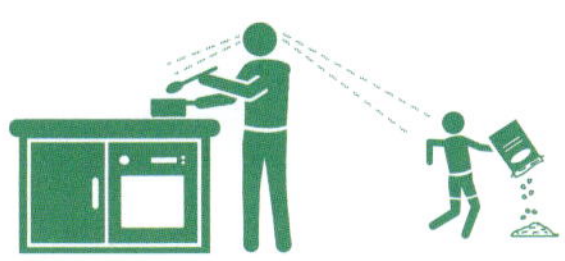

2 When you're a parent, you need to ______________________ !

5 Maureen was ______________________ before her wedding.

16 War and weapons

16.1 IDIOMS USING VOCABULARY ABOUT WAR AND WEAPONS

I have an ax to grind with my roommate. She's always playing loud music at night.

a grievance or dispute to take up

I decided to hold fire before booking such an expensive holiday. (UK)

wait before taking action

What has been going on while we were away? It's like a war zone in here!

very messy and chaotic

Buying a house can be a minefield. There's always so much to think about!

a complicated process with lots of potential problems

Balwant had to bite the bullet and tell his teacher that he hadn't done his homework.

do something nerve-wracking

Sonia stuck to her guns and told her daughter that she couldn't go to the party.

didn't change her mind when faced with conflict

Our daughter dropped a bombshell when she told us she and her new boyfriend were engaged.

delivered some shocking news

I always end up crossing swords with my grandfather when we talk about what's happening in the news.

arguing

Trying to make my children eat more vegetables has been an uphill battle.

a difficult struggle

My boss didn't give me a promotion, and then twisted the knife when she said my report was full of mistakes.

said or did something that made a bad situation feel worse

Poor you! You've really been in the wars! (UK)

suffered several injuries or misfortunes

They were so angry with each other that they almost came to blows!

had a fight or serious argument

The boss is in a terrible mood today! We're all going to be in the line of fire. (US)

likely to be criticized or punished (often unfairly)

I have some very bad news, but please don't shoot the messenger!

don't be angry with someone who reports bad news

Audrey looks really stressed. I think I dodged a bullet when she got that promotion and I didn't.

unintentionally avoided a situation that turned out to be bad

Jerry is a loose cannon. We should never have invited him to dinner with the clients.

someone who behaves unpredictably, often with bad consequences

My supervisor stabbed me in the back when she reported me to the store manager. I thought she was happy with my work.

betrayed me

I'm going to take my lunch break now. Could you hold down the fort until I get back? (US)

take care of something while someone is away

I lost my phone when I was shopping. It's a long shot, but I'm going to ask if anyone has handed it in at the store.

an attempt that has only a small chance of success

My girlfriend caught me off guard when she said two of her friends would be joining us for dinner tonight.

surprised me with something that I wasn't ready to deal with

Aa 16.2 MATCH THE BEGINNINGS OF THE SENTENCES TO THE CORRECT ENDINGS

I have an ax to grind with my roommate. → She's always playing loud music at night.

1. They were so angry with each other
2. I decided to hold fire before
3. The boss is in a terrible mood today!
4. Poor you!
5. I have some very bad news,

- that they almost came to blows!
- We're all going to be in the line of fire.
- She's always playing loud music at night.
- booking such an expensive holiday.
- but please don't shoot the messenger!
- You've really been in the wars!

16.3 LISTEN TO THE AUDIO AND MARK THE CORRECT PICTURE FOR EACH SENTENCE YOU HEAR

A ☐ B ☐ C ☑

1 

A ☐ B ☐ C ☐

2 

A ☐ B ☐ C ☐

3 

A ☐ B ☐ C ☐

4 

A ☐ B ☐ C ☐

5 

A ☐ B ☐ C ☐

Aa 16.4 CROSS OUT THE INCORRECT WORDS IN EACH SENTENCE

Trying to make my children eat more vegetables has been an uphill **battle** / ~~**fight**~~ / ~~**war**~~.

1  Balwant had to bite the **gun** / **bullet** / **sword** and tell his teacher that he hadn't done his homework.

2  Buying a house can be a **bombshell** / **battle** / **minefield**. There's always so much to think about!

3  I'm going to take my lunch break now. Could you hold down the **fort** / **castle** / **moat** until I get back?

4  Our daughter dropped a **minefield** / **bomb** / **bombshell** when she told us she and her new boyfriend were engaged.

5  Sonia stuck to her **swords** / **guns** / **bombs** and told her daughter that she couldn't go to the party.

Aa 16.5 WRITE THE CORRECT IDIOM NEXT TO ITS DEFINITION, FILLING IN THE MISSING LETTERS

delivered some shocking news = d r o p p e d a b o m b s h e l l

1 betrayed me = s _ _ _ _ _ _ m _ i _ t _ _ b _ _ _

2 a difficult struggle = a _ u _ _ _ _ _ b _ _ _ _ _

3 arguing = c _ _ _ _ _ _ _ s _ _ _ _ _

4 very messy and chaotic = l _ _ _ a w _ _ z _ _ _

5 a grievance or dispute to take up = a _ a _ t _ g _ _ _ _

17 Amount and distance

17.1 AMOUNT

What we've saved is just a drop in the ocean compared to what we need.

a tiny amount

Kaitlin's received stacks of letters from the bank, but hasn't opened them.

a large number of

We always take everything but the kitchen sink when we travel.

almost all our belongings

The Olympic swimming team has won tons of medals.

a large number of

I'll give you a thousand-and-one reasons why you shouldn't buy that house.

a huge number of

Rajesh has won every possible award for his movies, give or take one or two.

plus or minus; apart from

The guests began to arrive at the party in dribs and drabs.

slowly and in small numbers

Sam bought his brother's business, lock, stock, and barrel.

every part of something

Customers were few and far between because of the rain.

small in number; scarce

I'm so tired. I got precious little sleep last night.

almost no

17.2 DISTANCE

Carla's school is just a stone's throw away from the bus stop.

a short distance

The castle is in a far-flung corner of the island. It takes hours to drive there.

a distant, inaccessible part

The car avoided hitting my bike by just a hair's breadth.

a very short distance

The forest stretched as far as the eye can see.

into the distance

My new apartment is within walking distance of my workplace.

close enough to walk to from

You don't need to drive to the store. It's just around the corner.

a short distance away

People came from far and wide to watch the rock concert.

long distances away

I love to travel off the beaten path when I'm on vacation. (US)

to places that are less popular or difficult to reach

Jennifer won the marathon by a whisker.

by a very small amount or distance

Sharon lives in the middle of nowhere. You can't get there by train.

a place that is difficult to get to

Aa 17.3 MATCH THE BEGINNINGS OF THE IDIOMS TO THE CORRECT ENDINGS

just around →	the kitchen sink
1 a drop	of nowhere
2 the middle	the corner
3 everything but	beaten path
4 off the	in the ocean
5 in dribs	little
6 precious	and drabs

17.4 LISTEN TO THE AUDIO, THEN NUMBER THE PICTURES IN THE ORDER YOU HEAR THEM

A ☐

B *1*

C ☐

D ☐

E ☐

F ☐

Aa 17.5 REWRITE THE SENTENCES, CORRECTING THE ERRORS

The car avoided hitting my bike by just **a hair's width**.
The car avoided hitting my bike by just a hair's breadth.

1 The guests began to arrive at the party **in drips and drabs**.

____

2 My new apartment is **within running distance of** my workplace.

____

3 We always take **everything but the bathroom sink** when we travel.

____

4 The castle is in **a far-thrown corner** of the island. It takes hours to drive there.

____

5 Sharon lives in **the center of nowhere**. You can't get there by train.

____

Aa 17.6 MATCH THE PICTURES TO THE CORRECT SENTENCES

1 

2 

3 

4 

- Carla's school is just a stone's throw away from the bus stop.
- What we've saved is just a drop in the ocean compared to what we need.
- You don't need to drive to the store. It's just around the corner.
- The forest stretched as far as the eye can see.
- The Olympic swimming team has won tons of medals.

Aa 17.7 WRITE THE CORRECT IDIOM NEXT TO ITS DEFINITION

slowly and in small numbers = *in dribs and drabs*

1 a place that is difficult to get to = ____________

2 long distances away = ____________

3 a huge number of = ____________

4 small in number; scarce = ____________

5 easy to walk to from = ____________

6 by a very small amount or distance = ____________

7 almost all our belongings = ____________

18 Beginning and ending

18.1 BEGINNING

Mike's **made a fresh start** this year. He's eating much more healthily.

started to live life in a much better way

The sales team has **hit the ground running** since we launched our new smartphone.

done something with lots of enthusiasm right from the start

The New Year's celebrations **kicked off** with a band playing rock music.

began

Sophie's café finally **got off the ground** when she lowered her prices.

started to become successful

Tim's **turned over a new leaf**. He used to watch TV in the evenings, but now he goes jogging.

started to behave in a better way

The soccer team made **a promising start** to the season, beating last year's winners.

a beginning that shows lots of potential

The pottery course was far too difficult for **a newbie** like me.

someone starting an activity or a job for the first time

Mia's fashion firm **got off to a flying start**. She has already won three awards.

began extremely well

Let's **get the ball rolling**! Here's a brush and some paint for you.

start doing something with enthusiasm

I need to **get going** on the dinner. The guests are arriving in an hour!

start doing something immediately

18.2 ENDING

After selling the last sandwich, Dean decided to call it a day.

stop working

My cake's going to be great. I'm just putting the finishing touches on it. (US)

adding the final details to it

As the day drew to a close, we collected our things and left the beach.

came closer to its end

Trains across the city ground to a halt because of the snow.

slowed down and stopped

18.3 EXPRESSIONS WITH "END"

Jen is campaigning to put an end to the sale of plastic bottles.

make something end or stop happening

It was the end of an era when our boss retired after 30 years.

an important event that marks the end of a period of time

My vacation in Bali was so relaxing, but all good things must come to an end.

nothing lasts forever

A tasty pizza after a day of sightseeing provided the perfect end to a perfect day.

the ideal way to finish a good day

I've been marking tests all day, but the end is in sight!

it will be over soon

Winning the best actor award was a fitting end to Goro's career.

an appropriate way to end something

Aa 18.4 CROSS OUT THE INCORRECT WORDS IN EACH SENTENCE

Let's get the ball **rolling** / ~~**running**~~ / ~~**falling**~~! Here's a brush and some paint for you.

1  My cake's going to be great. I'm just putting the **ending** / **closing** / **finishing** touches on it.

2  The pottery course was far too difficult for a **startie** / **newbie** / **newie** like me.

3  Mike's made a **fresh** / **clean** / **cool** start this year. He's eating much more healthily.

4  I've been marking tests all day, but the end is in **view** / **reach** / **sight**!

18.5 LISTEN TO THE AUDIO AND MARK WHETHER THE SPEAKER IS TALKING ABOUT A BEGINNING OR AN ENDING

beginning ☐ ending ☑

1 beginning ☐ ending ☐

2 beginning ☐ ending ☐

3 beginning ☐ ending ☐

4 beginning ☐ ending ☐

5 beginning ☐ ending ☐

Aa 18.6 FILL IN THE GAPS, PUTTING THE WORDS IN THE CORRECT ORDER

perfect | the | day | a | perfect | end | to

A tasty pizza after a day of sightseeing provided *the perfect end to a perfect day.*

off | flying | a | to | start | got

1. Mia's fashion firm ___ ___ ___ ___ ___ ___ . She has already won three awards.

end | the | era | an | of

2. It was ___ ___ ___ ___ ___ when our boss retired after 30 years.

day | it | call | a

3. After selling the last sandwich, Dean decided to ___ ___ ___ ___ .

off | ground | the | got

4. Sophie's café finally ___ ___ ___ ___ when she lowered her prices.

halt | a | ground | to

5. Trains across the city ___ ___ ___ ___ because of the snow.

Aa 18.7 WRITE THE CORRECT IDIOM NEXT TO ITS DEFINITION, FILLING IN THE MISSING LETTERS

slowed down and stopped = *g r o u n d t o a h a l t*

1. an appropriate way to end something = a f _ _ _ _ _ _ e _ _
2. stop working = c _ _ _ i _ a d _ _
3. began = k _ _ _ _ _ o _ _
4. start doing something immediately = g _ _ g _ _ _ _
5. came closer to its end = d _ _ _ t _ a c _ _ _ _

19 Chance, luck, and probability

19.1 EXPRESSIONS WITH "CHANCE"

I think you'll need to replace your washing machine, but I'll take a look on the off-chance that I can fix it.

in the unlikely event

There was only a slim chance that we'd see a cheetah, so we were amazed when we spotted one.

a small possibility

The weather forecaster announced that we're in for a chance of rain tomorrow.

fairly likely to experience

We don't stand a chance of getting into the museum before lunchtime.

have no chance

19.2 EXPRESSIONS WITH "LUCK"

Winning the lottery was a stroke of luck for us.

something good that happens by chance

It was just a case of beginner's luck when I won that card game. I'd never played it before.

good luck for someone who has begun a new activity

I've already bought you ice cream. Don't push your luck!

Don't ask for anything else.

You're in luck! We have one dress left in your size.

lucky or able to do something

I'm afraid you're out of luck. The last train has just left the station.

unlucky or unable to do something

I hadn't studied for my tests, so it was sheer luck when I passed them.

very good luck that has nothing to do with planning or effort

19.3 PROBABILITY

Buster is the hot favourite to win the dog show. (UK)

the most likely to win

It looks like a medal is in the cards for Noriko after that amazing throw. (US)

a strong possibility

The result of the experiment is a foregone conclusion.

almost certain

Isabella says she will pass her English test, but don't hold your breath!

it is unlikely

Kerry will only clean up her room when pigs fly! (US)

never; it is very unlikely

I think Ruben's dreams of becoming a pop star are totally pie in the sky.

unrealistic or unlikely to happen

It's anyone's guess which player will win the game. They're both superb.

impossible to predict

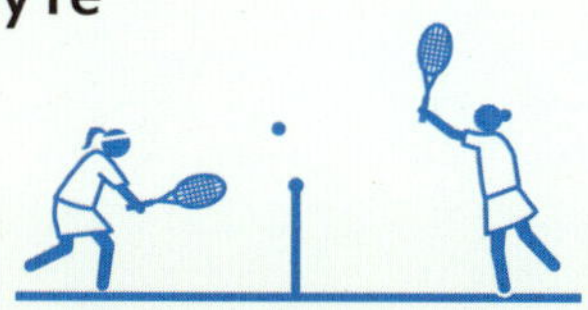

I had an interview for a great job, but blew it when I arrived half an hour late.

made something good much less likely to happen

Against all odds, Ryder completed his round-the-world sailing trip today.

despite circumstances that made it unlikely

Russell has injured his knee. It's touch-and-go whether he'll be able to play in the tournament this month.

very uncertain

Aa 19.4 READ THE STATEMENTS AND MARK THE CORRECT MEANING

I've already bought you ice cream. Don't push your luck!

You're lucky. ☐
You're unlucky. ☐
Don't ask for anything else. ☑

1. The weather forecaster announced that we're in for a chance of rain tomorrow.

Rain is very likely. ☐
Rain is fairly likely. ☐
Rain is very unlikely. ☐

2. Buster is the hot favourite to win the dog show.

Buster is likely to win. ☐
Buster is unlikely to win. ☐
Buster is too hot. ☐

3. Kerry will only clean up her room when pigs fly!

It is very likely. ☐
It might happen. ☐
It is very unlikely. ☐

4. Isabella says she will pass her English test, but don't hold your breath!

She will definitely pass. ☐
She is unlikely to pass. ☐
She has already failed. ☐

5. The result of the experiment is a foregone conclusion.

We already know it. ☐
We can't predict it. ☐
It is almost certain. ☐

Aa 19.5 MATCH THE PICTURES TO THE CORRECT SENTENCES

1 

2 

3 

4 

5 

It looks like a medal is in the cards for Noriko after that amazing throw.

The weather forecaster announced that we're in for a chance of rain tomorrow.

We don't stand a chance of getting into the museum before lunchtime.

I think Ruben's dreams of becoming a pop star are totally pie in the sky.

You're in luck! We have one dress left in your size.

I'm afraid you're out of luck. The last train has just left the station.

19.6 LISTEN TO THE AUDIO AND COMPLETE THE SENTENCES THAT DESCRIBE EACH PICTURE

It's *anyone's guess* which player will win the game. They're both superb.

1. It was just a case of ______________ when I won that card game. I'd never played it before.

2. There was only ______________ that we'd see a cheetah, so we were amazed when we spotted one.

3. Russell has injured his knee. It's ______________ ______________ whether he'll be able to play in the tournament this month.

4. I hadn't studied for my tests, so it was ______________ ______________ when I passed them.

5. I had an interview for a great job, but ______________ ______________ when I arrived half an hour late.

19.7 WRITE THE CORRECT IDIOM NEXT TO ITS DEFINITION

made something good much less likely to happen = *blew it*

1. in the unlikely event = ______________
2. despite circumstances that made it unlikely = ______________
3. something good that happens by chance = ______________
4. Don't ask for anything else. = ______________
5. the most likely to win = ______________

20 Ease and difficulty

20.1 EASE

The test was a cinch. I finished it 20 minutes early.

extremely easy

Getting around my city is a breeze. Our trains are excellent.

easy

Winning that race was like shooting fish in a barrel. Nobody else had trained.

very easy (usually about overcoming competition)

It's all too easy to forget to turn off the lights when you go out.

very easy (usually about a mistake)

Making a great cup of coffee is not rocket science.

not very complicated or difficult

Finding Angela's house was easy peasy. I have a GPS.

easy

I already play the violin, so learning the cello was a walk in the park.

easy

Unclogging my sink was a piece of cake for Carlita. She's a plumber.

extremely easy and straightforward

Alicia's worked in this factory so long she could do her job with her eyes shut.

easily, or without thinking

Driving on the left was difficult at first, but soon it was smooth sailing. (US)

easy, without major problems

20.2 DIFFICULTIES AND PROBLEMS

Doing the dishes after a dinner party is a pain in the neck.

very annoying or problematic

My home improvements opened a can of worms. The builders discovered so many problems.

caused a situation that leads to more difficulties

Don't make a mountain out of a molehill. I only asked you to help me bake a cake!

make a small task or problem seem bigger than it is

The team has a mountain to climb if it wants to win the game.

a huge amount to do, or problem to overcome

Giving up chocolate is easier said than done.

not as easy as it seems

Finishing the building this month is going to be a tall order.

very difficult

I was like a fish out of water at the science fiction convention.

in a difficult or unusual situation

There have been teething problems with the new computer system at work. (UK)

problems at the beginning of a process

Bashir was totally out of his depth on his first day working at the florist.

in a situation that is too difficult

I tried to make the politician answer my question, but it was like getting blood from a stone. (UK)

extremely difficult, usually because of someone's behavior

20.3 LISTEN TO THE AUDIO, THEN NUMBER THE SENTENCES IN THE ORDER YOU HEAR THEM

A  The test was a cinch. I finished it 20 minutes early. ☐

B  It's all too easy to forget to turn off the lights when you go out. ☐

C  Alicia's worked in this factory so long she could do her job with her eyes shut. ☐

D  Making a great cup of coffee is not rocket science. [1]

E  Finding Angela's house was easy peasy. I have a GPS. ☐

20.4 MARK THE SENTENCES THAT ARE CORRECT

I already play the violin, so learning the cello was a walk in the street. ☐
I already play the violin, so learning the cello was a walk in the park. ☑

1. There have been teething problems with the new computer system at work. ☐
   There have been toothing problems with the new computer system at work. ☐

2. Unclogging my sink was a slice of cake for Carlita. She's a plumber. ☐
   Unclogging my sink was a piece of cake for Carlita. She's a plumber. ☐

3. Doing the dishes after a dinner party is a pain in the head. ☐
   Doing the dishes after a dinner party is a pain in the neck. ☐

4. Getting around my city is a wind. Our trains are excellent. ☐
   Getting around my city is a breeze. Our trains are excellent. ☐

5. Finishing the building this month is going to be a tall order. ☐
   Finishing the building this month is going to be a high order. ☐

Aa 20.5 WRITE THE IDIOMS FROM THE PANEL IN THE CORRECT GROUPS

EASE	DIFFICULTY
smooth sailing	

easier said than done ~~smooth sailing~~ like shooting fish in a barrel out of his depth
a breeze a tall order with her eyes shut like getting blood from a stone

Aa 20.6 LOOK AT THE PICTURES AND COMPLETE THE SENTENCES

Bashir was totally *out of his depth* on his first day working at the florist.

3 The team has ______________________ ______________ if it wants to win the game.

1 Don't ______________________ .
I only asked you to help me bake a cake!

4 I was ______________________
at the science fiction convention.

2 My home improvements ______________ .
The builders discovered so many problems.

5 Doing the dishes after a dinner party is ________ ______________ .

21 Safety and danger

21.1 SAFETY

It might rain later. I'll play it safe and take an umbrella.

avoid any unnecessary risks

The rescue team found the climbers safe and sound after a week-long search.

unharmed and safe

Make sure you wear a helmet when you're cycling! Remember, safety first!

safety is the most important thing

Zahira is an excellent scuba teacher. You're in safe hands with her.

in the care of someone responsible

21.2 RISK AND DANGER

The route through the jungle was fraught with danger.

full of danger

That bike almost hit me! It was too close for comfort.

dangerously close

Elsa's job at the café is hanging by a thread after she dropped another tray of drinks.

in a very dangerous or insecure situation

You're skating on thin ice, Dai. You've arrived late for school every day this week.

potentially getting into trouble

If you don't do your violin practice, you run the risk of failing your test next week.

put yourself at risk

Blake is teetering on the brink of losing his job. His boss has given him a final warning.

close to a dangerous situation

The bear had left, and the coast was clear. We could continue with our trek.

it was safe to do something

After the crash, I called my mom to tell her I was still in one piece.

unharmed or uninjured

Are you sure you want to buy that motorcycle? I think you should look before you leap.

think about the consequences of taking risks

I always wear goggles when I do an experiment. Better safe than sorry!

Be careful so that you avoid problems later.

You have to take your life in your hands every time you cross this road.

take a great risk

I advised Kathy not to go into the water. It would be risking life and limb.

extremely dangerous

Hayley had a close shave. That ball almost hit her!

a situation where something bad nearly happened

Marco had a narrow escape, but managed to avoid being hit by the truck.

nearly had an accident, or got into danger

Jill's operation went well, but she's not out of the woods yet.

not out of danger

Maddy caught the train by the skin of her teeth. It left a few seconds later.

by the smallest possible amount of time

21.3 REWRITE THE SENTENCES, CORRECTING THE ERRORS

After the crash, I called my mom to tell her I was still **in one bit**.

After the crash, I called my mom to tell her I was still in one piece.

1. Zahira is an excellent scuba teacher. You're **in safe arms** with her.

2. Hayley had **a near shave**. That ball almost hit her!

3. I advised Kathy not to go into the water. It would be **risking life and leg**.

4. The bear had left, and **the ocean was clear**. We could continue with our trek.

21.4 LISTEN TO THE AUDIO AND MARK WHETHER THE SPEAKER IS TALKING ABOUT SAFETY OR DANGER

safety ☐
danger ☑

1. safety ☐
danger ☐

2. safety ☐
danger ☐

3. safety ☐
danger ☐

4. safety ☐
danger ☐

5. safety ☐
danger ☐

6. safety ☐
danger ☐

7. safety ☐
danger ☐

8. safety ☐
danger ☐

9. safety ☐
danger ☐

Aa 21.5 MATCH THE PICTURES TO THE CORRECT SENTENCES

❶ 

❷ 

❸ 

❹ 

❺ 

The rescue team found the climbers safe and sound after a week-long search.

Elsa's job at the café is hanging by a thread after she dropped another tray of drinks.

You have to take your life in your hands every time you cross this road.

Maddy caught the train by the skin of her teeth. It left a few seconds later.

The route through the jungle was fraught with danger.

Make sure you wear a helmet when you're cycling! Remember, safety first!

Aa 21.6 WRITE THE CORRECT IDIOM NEXT TO ITS DEFINITION

think about the consequences of taking risks = *look before you leap*

❶ unharmed or uninjured = ______

❷ nearly had an accident, or got into danger = ______

❸ safety is the most important thing = ______

❹ in the care of someone responsible = ______

❺ dangerously close = ______

22 Difficult situations

22.1 PROBLEMS AND DIFFICULTIES

Oh, no, I've missed the last bus home. I'm really in a jam now.

in a difficult situation

Logan's restaurant is in dire straits. There are never any customers.

in a very bad situation

Getting to work today was a nightmare. All the trains were canceled.

very difficult or unpleasant

The police officer came up against a brick wall when he asked if there were any witnesses to the crime.

couldn't make any progress

Not being able to read music was a stumbling block when I started learning the saxophone.

something that causes problems and stops progress

I'm in a bit of a tight spot because my boss has just asked me to work late tonight and it's my wedding anniversary.

in a difficult or awkward situation

I hated working at the diner. The final straw was when they made me dress as a chicken.

the last in a series of events that makes a bad situation impossible to tolerate

The peeling wallpaper was just the tip of the iceberg. The house needed so many repairs.

a small, visible part of a larger problem

Rosa was thrown in at the deep end when she had to teach the worst class in the school on her first day at work.

put in a difficult situation with no time to prepare

Tina was in a no-win situation. Her son wanted a beach vacation, but her daughter wanted to go skiing.

a difficult situation with no possibility of a positive outcome

Lisa has had **a bumpy ride** recently. First she broke her arm, and now she has failed her tests.

a difficult time

When Ava told me how much fun she'd had at the party, it **rubbed salt into the wound**. I wasn't invited.

made a bad situation feel worse

I have been offered a more interesting job, but the pay is terrible. I'm **caught between a rock and a hard place**.

facing a choice between two bad options

If you let your children eat whatever they want for dinner, you're **making a rod for your own back**. (UK)

causing yourself more difficulties in the future

The protesters want to stop the building being demolished, but they're **fighting a losing battle**.

trying to achieve something that is very unlikely

22.2 DEALING WITH PROBLEMS

I hate going to the dentist, but I know I have to **grin and bear it**.

accept a bad situation without complaining

Getting the old gramophone record player to work was **a tough nut to crack**.

a difficult problem to solve

The plumber **got to the bottom of** what's causing the leak. We need to replace the pipe.

found out what is causing a problem or situation

I can't believe you've upset your sister again! I'm the one who has to **pick up the pieces**.

try to make a situation better after something bad has happened

Working on the farm meant I had to **come to grips with** driving a tractor. (US)

learn how to do something challenging

22.3 MATCH THE BEGINNINGS OF THE IDIOMS TO THE CORRECT ENDINGS

	came up against → a brick wall	losing battle
1	a tough nut	bear it
2	fighting a	a brick wall
3	rubbed salt	to crack
4	grin and	the pieces
5	thrown in at	into the wound
6	pick up	the deep end

22.4 LISTEN TO THE AUDIO AND MARK THE IDIOMS YOU HEAR

A in dire straits ☐

B a stumbling block ✓

C the final straw ☐

D caught between a rock and a hard place ☐

E making a rod for your own back ☐

F a bumpy ride ☐

G a no-win situation ☐

H grin and bear it ☐

I in a bit of a tight spot ☐

22.5 CROSS OUT THE INCORRECT WORDS IN EACH SENTENCE

I hate going to the dentist, but I know I have to ~~smile~~ / grin / ~~laugh~~ and bear it.

1 

Oh, no, I've missed the last bus home. I'm really in a jam / trap / hole now.

2 

Working on the farm meant I had to come to hands / holds / grips with driving a tractor.

3 

The peeling wallpaper was just the tip / top / end of the iceberg. The house needed so many repairs.

4 

I hated working at the diner. The final line / straw / rope was when they made me dress as a chicken.

5 

The plumber got to the base / depth / bottom of what's causing the leak. We need to replace the pipe.

Aa 22.6 FILL IN THE GAPS USING THE IDIOMS IN THE PANEL

Logan's restaurant is *in dire straits*. There are never any customers.

1 Not being able to read music was ______________________ when I started learning the saxophone.

2 The protesters want to stop the building being demolished, but they're ______________________.

3 If you let your children eat whatever they want for dinner, you're ______________________.

4 I hate going to the dentist, but I know I have to ______________________.

5 I can't believe you've upset your sister again! I'm the one who has to ______________________.

fighting a losing battle	~~in dire straits~~	pick up the pieces
a stumbling block	making a rod for your own back	grin and bear it

Aa 22.7 WRITE THE CORRECT IDIOM NEXT TO ITS DEFINITION, FILLING IN THE MISSING LETTERS

learn how to do something challenging = c *o m e* t *o* g *r i p s* w *i t h*

1 very difficult or unpleasant = a n _ _ _ _ _ _ _ _

2 a difficult time = a b _ _ _ _ r _ _ _

3 in a very bad situation = i _ d _ _ _ s _ _ _ _ _ _

4 a difficult problem to solve = a t _ _ _ _ n _ _ t _ c _ _ _ _

5 in a difficult situation = i _ a j _ _

23 The weather and nature

23.1 DESCRIBING THE WEATHER

Nina always takes her dog for a walk **come rain or shine**.

whatever the weather

Are you sure you want to go for a walk? There's **a howling wind** out there! (US)

a very strong wind

It's **raining cats and dogs**. I wish I hadn't forgotten my umbrella.

raining heavily

You don't need a coat, Phil! It's **like an oven** outside.

extremely hot

We had to leave the beach because it started **bucketing down**. (UK)

raining heavily

What **a scorcher**! It's perfect weather for a barbecue.

a very hot and sunny day

23.3 IDIOMS USING VOCABULARY ABOUT NATURE

There are lots of cafés and restaurants in **my neck of the woods**.

my local area

After months of boring lessons, our new teacher was **a breath of fresh air**.

an exciting change for the better

Don't be such **a stick-in-the-mud**! If you try skydiving, you might enjoy it.

someone who is unwilling to try new things

This politician used to be really popular, but now **the tide has turned**.

circumstances or people's opinions are the opposite of what they used to be

23.2 IDIOMS USING VOCABULARY ABOUT THE WEATHER

I love looking after my niece. She's a ray of sunshine.

a cheerful person who makes you feel happy

I had five minutes' peace before my students arrived. It was the calm before the storm.

the quiet period before a time of trouble or excitement

Isaac and Fatima's argument about which movie to watch was just a storm in a teacup.

an argument or controversy about something unimportant

Sorry, but we'll have to take a rain check on meeting up tonight. I'm not feeling very well.

postpone or cancel

You weren't listening to me, were you? You had your head in the clouds.

were thinking about something else

Megan stole my thunder when she told the professor the result of my experiment.

stole my idea, or diverted attention away from me

I wish my boss would stop beating around the bush and tell me what he really thinks of my product idea.

avoiding a subject by talking about irrelevant things

Kieran is so involved in every detail of this project that he can't see the forest for the trees. (US)

is looking too closely at the small details to see a whole situation clearly

I'm so tired tonight! I'm going to hit the hay. (US)

go to bed

The decision to close the library made waves in my local area.

caused controversy

Aa 23.4 MATCH THE PICTURES TO THE CORRECT SENTENCES

1 

2 

3 

We had to leave the beach because it started bucketing down.

It's raining cats and dogs. I wish I hadn't forgotten my umbrella.

Nina always takes her dog for a walk come rain or shine.

What a scorcher! It's perfect weather for a barbecue.

Aa 23.5 MARK THE SENTENCES THAT ARE CORRECT

I love looking after my niece. She's a ray of sunshine. ✓
I love looking after my niece. She's a beam of sunshine.

1. You weren't listening to me, were you? You had your head in the air.
   You weren't listening to me, were you? You had your head in the clouds.

2. This politician used to be really popular, but now the tide has turned.
   This politician used to be really popular, but now the ocean has turned.

3. Isaac and Fatima's argument about which movie to watch was just a cloud in a teacup.
   Isaac and Fatima's argument about which movie to watch was just a storm in a teacup.

4. You don't need a coat, Phil! It's like a fire outside.
   You don't need a coat, Phil! It's like an oven outside.

5. I'm so tired tonight! I'm going to hit the hay.
   I'm so tired tonight! I'm going to hit the grass.

6. There are lots of cafés and restaurants in my neck of the woods.
   There are lots of cafés and restaurants in my neck of the trees.

Aa 23.6 WRITE THE IDIOMS FROM THE PANEL UNDER THE CORRECT DEFINITIONS

go to bed

hit the hay

1. someone who is unwilling to try new things
2. a cheerful person who makes you feel happy
3. postpone or cancel
4. an exciting change for the better
5. a very strong wind
6. extremely hot
7. raining heavily

a ray of sunshine | raining cats and dogs | a breath of fresh air | like an oven | ~~hit the hay~~ | a howling wind | take a rain check on | a stick-in-the-mud

23.7 LISTEN TO THE AUDIO, THEN NUMBER THE PICTURES IN THE ORDER YOU HEAR THEM

A ☐

B ☐

C ☐

D *1*

E ☐

F ☐

G ☐

H ☐

24 Talking

24.1 EXPRESSIONS WITH "TALK"

Ahmed talks the talk, but isn't very hardworking.

talks in a convincing way

I've tried telling Maya to clean up her room, but it's like talking to a brick wall.

pointless because the other person won't respond

Ryan wants to join the circus. I'm trying to talk some sense into him.

persuade him to behave in a sensible way

Kirsty's always commenting on other people's clothes. She can talk!

She's just as bad herself!

My colleagues love to talk shop when they meet for lunch.

talk about their jobs

Linda likes to talk big. She claims she's visited every country.

boast or exaggerate

Leo can talk himself out of any awkward situation.

escape from any difficult situation using lies or humor

Tamara is really friendly, but she can talk your ear off.

talk at great length

I hate it when my boss talks down to me!

patronizes me

I made small talk with Marisha while we waited for the train.

polite conversation about unimportant or uncontroversial things

24.2 CONVERSATION AND TALKING

I always enjoy a chitchat with my sister over coffee. (US)

a chat or gossip

This politician has a reputation for speaking his mind.

saying exactly what he thinks about something

My grandpa spins a good yarn. He loves telling us about his childhood adventures.

tells funny or unlikely stories

The students parroted the facts without using their own words.

repeated word for word

Akio struck up a conversation with one of his fellow passengers.

began a conversation

I sat on the shore with my boyfriend, shooting the breeze. (US)

talking in a relaxed way

Nina keeps droning on about her new car. It's getting really boring!

talking at length in an uninteresting way

Sarah was born with the gift of the gab. She could sell you anything.

the ability to speak confidently and persuasively

My cousin is such a loudmouth. He never stops talking!

someone who talks too much

Cat got your tongue? You usually have so much to say.

You're being very quiet.

Aa 24.3 MATCH THE BEGINNINGS OF THE SENTENCES TO THE CORRECT ENDINGS

Akio struck up a conversation	without using their own words.
1 I always enjoy a chitchat	talks down to me!
2 The students parroted the facts	with one of his fellow passengers.
3 Ahmed talks the talk,	with my sister over coffee.
4 I hate it when my boss	but isn't very hardworking.
5 Leo can talk himself out	for speaking his mind.
6 My colleagues love to talk shop	but it's like talking to a brick wall.
7 This politician has a reputation	of any awkward situation.
8 I made small talk with Marisha	when they meet for lunch.
9 I've tried telling Maya to clean up her room,	while we waited for the train.

Aa 24.4 WRITE THE CORRECT IDIOM NEXT TO ITS DEFINITION, FILLING IN THE MISSING LETTERS

a chat or gossip	=	a chitchat
1 talk about their jobs	=	t _ _ _ s _ _ _
2 tells funny or unlikely stories	=	s _ _ _ _ a g _ _ _ y _ _ _
3 She's just as bad herself!	=	S _ _ c _ _ t _ _ _ !
4 boast or exaggerate	=	t _ _ _ b _ _
5 repeated word for word	=	p _ _ _ _ _ _ _
6 patronizes me	=	t _ _ _ _ d _ _ _ t _ m _
7 talks in a convincing way	=	t _ _ _ _ t _ _ t _ _ _

24.5 LISTEN TO THE AUDIO AND MARK THE IDIOMS YOU HEAR

struck up a conversation ☐	speaking his mind ☐	shooting the breeze ☑
1 talk some sense into him ☐	talks down to me ☐	She can talk! ☐
2 speaking his mind ☐	spins a good yarn ☐	talk your ear off ☐
3 the gift of the gab ☐	droning on ☐	a loudmouth ☐
4 talks down to me ☐	talks the talk ☐	small talk ☐

24.6 LOOK AT THE PICTURES AND COMPLETE THE SENTENCES USING THE IDIOMS IN THE PANEL

Ryan wants to join the circus. I'm trying to *talk some sense into him* .

1 Nina keeps ________________ about her new car. It's getting really boring!

2 This politician has a reputation for ________________ .

3 Sarah was born with ________________ . She could sell you anything.

4 ________________ You usually have so much to say.

5 I sat on the shore with my boyfriend, ________________ .

speaking his mind	Cat got your tongue?	~~talk some sense into him~~
shooting the breeze	droning on	the gift of the gab

25 Sharing information

25.1 SHARING NEWS

Good luck with your interview today. **Keep me posted** about how it goes!

keep me informed with the latest news

Rumors that the two actors had secretly gotten married **spread like wildfire**.

spread very quickly

Anna's manager **touched base** with her for a quick update on her research.

had a brief conversation to get an update

Angie **filled me in** on what happened at work while I was away.

told me all the latest important information

This restaurant couldn't afford an advertising campaign, but it has become really popular **by word of mouth**.

by people talking about it

We must have **got our wires crossed**. I thought the dress code for this party was casual.

misunderstood information, or become confused

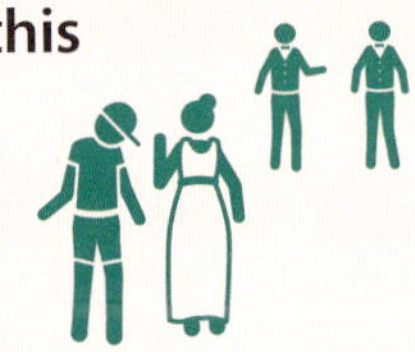

25.2 IDIOMS USING VOCABULARY ABOUT ANIMALS

Pedro's going to marry Elena. I **heard it from the horse's mouth**.

heard the news directly from the original source

A little bird told me that Richa is going to be promoted.

someone (whose name I won't reveal) told me

I'm planning a surprise trip to Paris with Liam to celebrate our wedding anniversary. Don't **let the cat out of the bag**!

reveal a secret by mistake

The boss **stirred up a hornet's nest** when she said we would have to take a pay cut. (US)

caused a lot of upset or excitement

I'm afraid your cat will have to stay here overnight, but I promise I'll **keep you in the picture** about how she's recovering.

keep you fully informed

Lin decided to **get it off her chest** and told Mel all about her relationship problems.

share something worrying or upsetting

The tour rep **broke the news** to us that our flight had been canceled.

revealed important (and usually bad) news

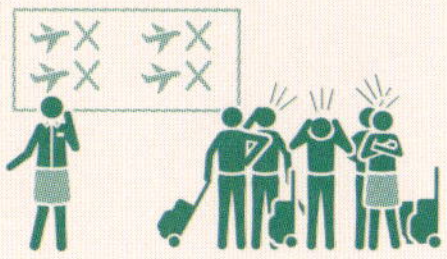

The design team make sure they always **keep me in the loop**.

keep me updated about shared information

I'm sorry to be **the bearer of bad news**, but we won't be able to fix your computer.

someone who delivers bad news

Phil showed me around the kitchen. He knows **the nuts and bolts** of running a restaurant.

the practical rules of something

25.3 IDIOMS USING VOCABULARY ABOUT FOOD

When news stories are shocking, I always **take them with a grain of salt.** (US)

don't completely believe them

I **heard it through the grapevine** that Luisa is pregnant.

heard some news through gossip or rumor

After leaving the band, Marco **dished the dirt** about the other band members to a journalist.

shared malicious gossip

Why did you **spill the beans** and tell Luke I had a new boyfriend? I wanted to tell him myself.

reveal a secret

25.4 LISTEN TO THE AUDIO, THEN NUMBER THE SENTENCES IN THE ORDER YOU HEAR THEM

A. Good luck with your interview today. Keep me posted about how it goes! ☐

B. The tour rep broke the news to us that our flight had been canceled. ☐

C. Phil showed me around the kitchen. He knows the nuts and bolts of running a restaurant. [1]

D. Pedro's going to marry Elena. I heard it from the horse's mouth. ☐

E. A little bird told me that Richa is going to be promoted. ☐

F. Angie filled me in on what happened at work while I was away. ☐

G. The design team make sure they always keep me in the loop. ☐

H. Lin decided to get it off her chest and told Mel all about her relationship problems. ☐

25.5 REWRITE THE SENTENCES, CORRECTING THE ERRORS

I'm sorry to be **the giver of bad news**, but we won't be able to fix your computer.

I'm sorry to be the bearer of bad news, but we won't be able to fix your computer.

1. We must have **got our lines crossed**. I thought the dress code for this party was casual.

2. When news stories are shocking, I always **take them with a grain of sugar**.

3. The boss **stirred up a bee's nest** when she said we would have to take a pay cut.

4. After leaving the band, Marco **served the dirt** about the other band members to a journalist.

5. Anna's manager **touched ground** with her for a quick update on her research.

6. The tour rep **smashed the news** to us that our flight had been canceled.

Aa 25.6 MATCH THE PICTURES TO THE CORRECT SENTENCES

This restaurant couldn't afford an advertising campaign, but it has become really popular by word of mouth.

1 

Lin decided to get it off her chest and told Mel all about her relationship problems.

2 

I'm afraid your cat will have to stay here overnight, but I promise I'll keep you in the picture about how she's recovering.

3 

Why did you spill the beans and tell Luke I had a new boyfriend? I wanted to tell him myself.

4 

Rumors that the two actors had secretly gotten married spread like wildfire.

5 

I'm planning a surprise trip to Paris with Liam to celebrate our wedding anniversary. Don't let the cat out of the bag!

Aa 25.7 WRITE THE CORRECT IDIOM NEXT TO ITS DEFINITION

keep me updated about shared information = *keep me in the loop*

1. someone who delivers bad news = __________
2. don't completely believe them = __________
3. misunderstood information, or become confused = __________
4. heard some news through gossip or rumor = __________
5. had a brief conversation to get an update = __________

26 Truth and lies

26.1 TELLING THE TRUTH

I'm scared of dogs. In fact, I'm terrified of them, **to tell you the truth**.

to be completely honest

Nathan **came clean** with his parents and told them he had broken the window.

confessed to doing something wrong

My teacher was **brutally honest** with me and told me my essay was terrible.

honest in a very direct or insensitive way

The voting process in this election is completely **above board**. All the votes are counted and checked.

honest, open, or legal

A whistleblower has told the authorities about the dirty conditions in the kitchen at work.

someone who tells a person in authority about something illegal or wrong

26.2 KEEPING SECRETS

Tania told me a secret but asked me to **keep it under my hat**.

avoid telling anyone

Anita's recipe for her banana cake is **top secret**. She won't share it with anyone.

completely secret

I promise I won't tell Lizzie you're going to propose to her. **My lips are sealed.**

I will keep it a secret.

I'm not going to tell you how much my house cost. It's **none of your business**!

private information

We're keeping our new car model **under wraps** until the launch later this week.

secret

26.3 TELLING LIES

I thought Bella's hat was ridiculous, but I told her **a white lie** and said I loved it.

a lie to avoid hurting someone's feelings

I think Warren was **bending the truth** when I interviewed him for this job. He said he had excellent IT skills.

lying, misleading people, or exaggerating

My wife was angry when I **went behind her back** and bought myself a new motorcycle.

did something without telling her

David **lied through his teeth** to his mom. He claimed the cat had broken her favorite vase.

told a blatant lie

The salesman really **took us for a ride** when he sold us this car. It's always breaking down!

deceived or cheated us

Our boss says the company is doing well, but she has a reputation for **telling half-truths**.

not telling the whole truth

26.4 SUSPICION

I **have a sneaking suspicion** that Marcia was at a job interview this morning.

suspect something without firm evidence

I knew Frida hadn't been out sick. I **smelled a rat** when she came back to work with a suntan.

suspected that someone had lied

The children are being very quiet. I think there's **something fishy** going on!

something suspicious

The piano teacher **had a hunch** that Jordan hadn't done any practice since his last lesson.

suspected

Aa 26.5 MARK THE SENTENCES THAT ARE CORRECT

Anita's recipe for her banana cake is high secret. She won't share it with anyone. ☐
Anita's recipe for her banana cake is top secret. She won't share it with anyone. ☑

1 

The children are being very quiet. I think there's something fishy going on! ☐
The children are being very quiet. I think there's something tricky going on! ☐

2 

Tania told me a secret but asked me to keep it under my coat. ☐
Tania told me a secret but asked me to keep it under my hat. ☐

3 

My wife was angry when I went behind her head and bought myself a new motorcycle. ☐
My wife was angry when I went behind her back and bought myself a new motorcycle. ☐

4 

I promise I won't tell Lizzie you're going to propose to her. My lips are sealed. ☐
I promise I won't tell Lizzie you're going to propose to her. My lips are closed. ☐

5 

I thought Bella's hat was ridiculous, but I told her a white lie and said I loved it. ☐
I thought Bella's hat was ridiculous, but I told her a pink lie and said I loved it. ☐

Aa 26.6 WRITE THE IDIOMS FROM THE PANEL IN THE CORRECT GROUPS

TRUTH	LIES
a whistleblower	

bending the truth ~~a whistleblower~~ telling half-truths came clean
above board went behind her back took us for a ride brutally honest

26.7 LISTEN TO THE AUDIO AND MARK THE IDIOMS YOU HEAR

- **A** lied through his teeth ☑
- **B** my lips are sealed ☐
- **C** to tell you the truth ☐
- **D** had a hunch ☐
- **E** under wraps ☐
- **F** bending the truth ☐
- **G** have a sneaking suspicion ☐

26.8 READ THE LETTER AND CROSS OUT THE INCORRECT WORDS

Hi Sunita,

I have some exciting news for you, but please keep it under / ~~below~~ your hat because it's most / top secret at the moment. I've been promoted! I had a hint / hunch that I would get the job because my interview went well. As I said, please don't tell anyone because my new boss still wants to keep it under wraps / cover.

Love, Lindsay

26.9 LOOK AT THE PICTURES AND COMPLETE THE SENTENCES USING THE IDIOMS IN THE PANEL

We're keeping our new car model *under wraps* until the launch later this week.

3 I knew Frida hadn't been out sick. I ______________ when she came back to work with a suntan.

1 I'm not going to tell you how much my house cost. It's ______________________________!

4 David ______________________ to his mom. He claimed the cat had broken her favorite vase.

2 ____________________ has told the authorities about the dirty conditions in the kitchen at work.

5 My teacher was ______________________ with me and told me my essay was terrible.

smelled a rat	none of your business	brutally honest
A whistleblower	~~under wraps~~	lied through his teeth

27 Looking and listening

27.1 LOOKING AND WATCHING

The examiner watched us like a hawk, making sure we didn't cheat.

watched us very carefully

Felipe cast a glance at his watch. The bus was already 10 minutes late.

looked quickly

Kezia looked furious when I told her I'd torn her dress. If looks could kill!

Someone looked very angry.

Bastian kept a close watch on his children as they played outside.

watched carefully

The teacher turned a blind eye to his students' bad behavior.

ignored, or pretended not to see

We kept our eyes peeled, hoping we'd spot some rare birds.

watched very carefully for something

I asked my brother to keep an eye on the dinner while I was talking on the phone.

take care of something, or watch something carefully

The border guard gave my documents the once-over, then let me drive on.

a quick check or inspection

I always cast an eye over my desk to make sure I haven't forgotten anything when I leave the office.

look at or check something quickly

Karen has an eagle eye. She found lots of mistakes when I asked her to check my essay.

the ability to spot small details

27.2 LISTENING AND HEARING

Jenny, please tell me how the interview went. I'm all ears!

I'm eager to hear about it!

I told my daughter she should work harder, but my advice fell on deaf ears.

was ignored

My grandfather is hard of hearing, so I often have to repeat things to him.

partially deaf

Omar lent a sympathetic ear when I broke up with my boyfriend.

listened to someone's problems with sympathy

Martina didn't hear the teacher's question. She was a million miles away.

not listening at all

Be careful what you say about the boss. Remember, walls have ears!

you never know who's listening when you're talking in a public place

I completely zoned out during that meeting. It was so boring!

stopped listening or concentrating

It was music to my ears when my son told me he'd passed his driving test.

wonderful news

Ethan was only listening with half an ear and kept checking his phone as I spoke to him.

not listening attentively

When my parents got wind of the fact that I'd had a house party, they were furious.

found out about something that was meant to be a secret

Aa 27.3 CROSS OUT THE INCORRECT WORDS IN EACH SENTENCE

I told my daughter she should work harder, but my advice fell on ~~closed~~ / ~~blocked~~ / **deaf** ears.

1. Felipe **cast** / **threw** / **looked** a glance at his watch. The bus was already 10 minutes late.
2. Jenny, please tell me how the interview went. I'm all **eyes** / **ears** / **listening**!
3. Bastian **kept** / **held** / **gave** a close watch on his children as they played outside.
4. The examiner watched us like a **bear** / **hawk** / **lion**, making sure we didn't cheat.
5. Kezia looked furious when I told her I'd torn her dress. If **looks** / **eyes** / **ears** could kill!
6. When my parents got **air** / **ear** / **wind** of the fact that I'd had a house party, they were furious.
7. Omar lent a **kind** / **sympathetic** / **nice** ear when I broke up with my boyfriend.

27.4 LISTEN TO THE AUDIO, THEN NUMBER THE PICTURES IN THE ORDER YOU HEAR THEM

A ☐

B [1]

C ☐

D ☐

E ☐

F ☐

G ☐

H ☐

I ☐

Aa 27.5 MATCH THE BEGINNINGS OF THE IDIOMS TO THE CORRECT ENDINGS

	a million → miles away	half an ear
1	If looks	hearing
2	hard of	miles away
3	listening with	could kill!
4	fell on	sympathetic ear
5	cast an	like a hawk
6	watched us	blind eye
7	lent a	eye over
8	turned a	deaf ears

Aa 27.6 MARK THE SENTENCES THAT ARE CORRECT

I asked my brother to put an eye on the dinner while I was talking on the phone. ☐
I asked my brother to keep an eye on the dinner while I was talking on the phone. ☑

1 

Be careful what you say about the boss. Remember, walls have ears! ☐
Be careful what you say about the boss. Remember, doors have ears! ☐

2 

We kept our eyes peeled, hoping we'd spot some rare birds. ☐
We kept our eyes alert, hoping we'd spot some rare birds. ☐

3 

Martina didn't hear the teacher's question. She was a thousand miles away. ☐
Martina didn't hear the teacher's question. She was a million miles away. ☐

4 

The border guard gave my documents the twice-over, then let me drive on. ☐
The border guard gave my documents the once-over, then let me drive on. ☐

5 

The teacher turned a blind eye to his students' bad behavior. ☐
The teacher turned a closed eye to his students' bad behavior. ☐

Aa 27.7 WRITE THE CORRECT IDIOM NEXT TO ITS DEFINITION, FILLING IN THE MISSING LETTERS

watched very carefully for something = k e p t o u r e y e s p e e l e d

1 wonderful news = m _ _ _ _ t _ m _ e _ _ _

2 the ability to spot small details = a _ e _ _ _ _ e _ _

3 look at or check something quickly = c _ _ _ a _ e _ _ o _ _ _

4 was ignored = f _ _ _ o _ d _ _ _ e _ _ _

5 partially deaf = h _ _ _ o _ h _ _ _ _ _ _

28 Music and the arts

28.1 IDIOMS USING VOCABULARY ABOUT MUSIC AND THE ARTS

How many times must I drum it into your head? Wipe your feet on the mat!

tell you something again and again

Our new bookstore opens today. Let's get the show on the road!

get something started or working properly

You've changed your tune! I thought you didn't like cats.

changed your opinion

Dennis broke his mom's laptop. He had to face the music and tell her.

accept the consequences of actions

Pavel decided to jazz up his house, so he painted it purple.

make something brighter, more colorful, or more exciting

Juanita is so careful at work. She does everything by the book.

follows the rules, or does things in the expected way

Isaac's speech at the wedding hit the right note. It was really funny, but no one was offended.

was appropriate, or the right thing to say

Making sure people know about our concert will help us drum up an audience.

get by making an effort

Ramona loves to toot her own horn. She's always showing us her trophies. (US)

talk too much about her achievements

When Fay told me about her engagement, it was music to my ears!

wonderful news

Dad's always telling me to clean my room. He is like a broken record.

says the same thing again and again

Ian's desserts are amazing. He'll be a tough act to follow when he leaves.

difficult to follow with as much success

The police chief put us in the picture about the bank robbery. (UK)

explained the facts about a situation

I knew it was Enzo who had eaten my lunch. I can read him like a book.

understand what he's thinking from his body language

I'm going to take a page out of your book and clean my desk. (US)

copy your good habit

Antonio is great at flower arranging. He has it down to an art.

is an expert in something, usually after much practice

Nisha is helping me fine-tune my presentation for tomorrow morning.

change something slightly to make it even better

Kira's boss made a scene when she arrived five minutes late.

made an unnecessary fuss

Arjun felt left out of the picture when his roommates got a dog without telling him.

not informed about some news or a situation

Despite the rain, we decided not to cancel the play in the park. The show must go on!

Something must still happen despite any difficulties.

28.2 LISTEN TO THE AUDIO AND MARK THE IDIOMS YOU HEAR

	music to my ears	☑	face the music	☐	made a scene	☐
1	drum up	☐	hit the right note	☐	face the music	☐
2	changed your tune	☐	music to my ears	☐	fine-tune	☐
3	a tough act to follow	☐	jazz up	☐	hit the right note	☐
4	toot her own horn	☐	left out of the picture	☐	The show must go on!	☐
5	changed your tune	☐	fine-tune	☐	music to my ears	☐
6	get the show on the road	☐	has it down to an art	☐	is like a broken record	☐
7	face the music	☐	read him like a book	☐	changed your tune	☐

28.3 REWRITE THE SENTENCES, CORRECTING THE ERRORS

Pavel decided to **rock up** his house, so he painted it purple.
Pavel decided to jazz up his house, so he painted it purple.

1. Antonio is great at flower arranging. He **has it down to a picture**.

2. Juanita is so careful at work. She **does everything by the story**.

3. I'm going to **take a chapter out of your book** and clean my desk.

4. The police chief **put us in the drawing** about the bank robbery.

5. How many times must I **shake it into your head**? Wipe your feet on the mat!

Aa 28.4 MATCH THE DEFINITIONS TO THE CORRECT IDIOMS

	Definitions	Idioms
	was appropriate, or the right thing to say → hit the right note	music to my ears
1	talk too much about her achievements	made a scene
2	wonderful news	hit the right note
3	get by making an effort	toot her own horn
4	made an unnecessary fuss	face the music
5	says the same thing again and again	drum up
6	accept the consequences of actions	is like a broken record

Aa 28.5 LOOK AT THE PICTURES AND COMPLETE THE SENTENCES

Ramona loves to *toot her own horn* .
She's always showing us her trophies.

3 You've ______________________ !
I thought you didn't like cats.

1 Ian's desserts are amazing. He'll be ____________
____________ when he leaves.

4 Nisha is helping me ______________________
my presentation for tomorrow morning.

2 Arjun felt ______________________
when his roommates got a dog without telling him.

5 Dennis broke his mom's laptop. He had to
______________________ and tell her.

29 Eating and drinking

29.1 EATING

Yuka's complaining that her sons have eaten her out of house and home.

eaten all the food in her house

Mario celebrated his 70th birthday with a feast fit for a king.

a delicious meal with lots of courses

The sight of the cake in the café window made my mouth water.

made me hungry, or want to eat something

Paolo was so hungry that he wolfed down that huge burger really quickly.

ate quickly and greedily

You can buy yourself a square meal at the student café for a few dollars.

a satisfying and nutritious meal

Aliyah whipped up an omelet for Caleb and his friends.

prepared a meal quickly

Ethan took his new client out for a sit-down meal. (US)

a large and tasty meal, usually in a restaurant

Krish always starts his day with a hearty breakfast.

a large breakfast

29.2 DRINKING

I washed down my pizza with a glass of lemonade.

followed a meal with a drink

Chris bought a round of drinks for the basketball team.

drinks you buy for the group of people you are with

Blue cheese is an acquired taste. I still think it's disgusting, but Joe loves it.

something that you only like after trying it a few times

I was in a rush, so I grabbed something to eat from the fast food stand.

bought something to eat in a hurry

Wayne eats like a bird. He only ever orders a small salad for lunch.

eats a very small amount

I'm so glad I ordered an extra-large pizza. I could eat a horse!

I feel extremely hungry.

Nigel took a tray of piping hot cupcakes out of the oven.

very hot

We complained to the waiter that our soup was stone cold.

completely cold

We sat in front of the TV stuffing our faces with popcorn.

eating lots of food in a greedy way

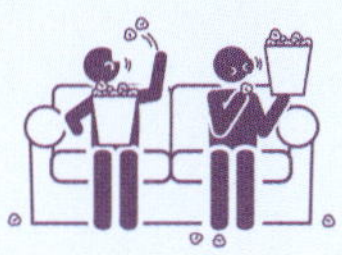

You shouldn't eat so many cookies! You'll spoil your appetite.

lose your desire to eat later

After three hours in the gym, Dan quenched his thirst with a glass of juice.

satisfied his thirst

I felt parched after working in the sun, so I drank a whole bottle of water.

extremely thirsty

Aa 29.3 MATCH THE PICTURES TO THE CORRECT SENTENCES

1 

2 

3 

4 

5 

6 

7 

8 

We sat in front of the TV stuffing our faces with popcorn.

Krish always starts his day with a hearty breakfast.

Ethan took his new client out for a sit-down meal.

You shouldn't eat so many cookies! You'll spoil your appetite.

Nigel took a tray of piping hot cupcakes out of the oven.

I washed down my pizza with a glass of lemonade.

Aliyah whipped up an omelet for Caleb and his friends.

We complained to the waiter that our soup was stone cold.

Mario celebrated his 70th birthday with a feast fit for a king.

29.4 LISTEN TO THE AUDIO AND MARK THE CORRECT PICTURE FOR EACH SENTENCE YOU HEAR

 A ☐  B ☐  C ☑

1  A ☐  B ☐  C ☐

2  A ☐  B ☐  C ☐

3  A ☐  B ☐  C ☐

4  A ☐  B ☐  C ☐

5  A ☐  B ☐  C ☐

Aa 29.5 FILL IN THE GAPS, PUTTING THE WORDS IN THE CORRECT ORDER

her | house | of | home | and | eaten | out

Yuka's complaining that her sons have *eaten* *her* *out* *of* *house* *and* *home*.

fit | king | a | for | feast | a

1 Mario celebrated his 70th birthday with ______ ______ ______ ______ ______ ______.

to | something | grabbed | eat

2 I was in a rush, so I ______ ______ ______ ______ from the fast food stand.

mouth | my | water | made

3 The sight of the cake in the café window ______ ______ ______ ______.

drinks | of | round | a

4 Chris bought ______ ______ ______ ______ for the basketball team.

could | a | horse! | I | eat

5 I'm so glad I ordered an extra-large pizza. ______ ______ ______ ______ ______

Aa 29.6 WRITE THE CORRECT IDIOM NEXT TO ITS DEFINITION

bought something to eat in a hurry = *grabbed something to eat*

1 a satisfying and nutritious meal = ______

2 eats a very small amount = ______

3 ate quickly and greedily = ______

4 prepared a meal quickly = ______

5 lose your desire to eat later = ______

30 Describing your health

30.1 SICKNESS AND RECOVERY

Leo was feeling the worse for wear after he stayed out all night.

tired or in a bad state

My hay fever tends to flare up every summer.

suddenly get worse

Ayano was feeling under the weather, so she left work early.

not well, slightly sick or ill

This music's far too loud! It has given me a splitting headache.

a terrible headache

I don't feel very well. I think I'm coming down with something.

starting to get sick

Pablo is on the road to recovery after breaking his leg.

getting better

30.2 HEALTH AND FITNESS

Ollie received a clean bill of health from his doctor.

the news that you are completely healthy

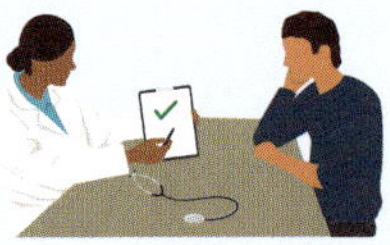

The dancers in this show have to be as fit as a fiddle.

very fit and healthy

After turning 40, Tom decided to get in shape and started jogging.

become fitter and healthier, usually by losing weight

Moving to the country has given Kira a new lease on life. (US)

new energy and enthusiasm for life

I'm not well enough to go to work today, so I'm going to **call in sick**.

call my employer to say I am too sick to work

Yuka fell and cut her leg really badly when she was hiking, but she's **on the mend** now.

getting better

Jeanne has **a heavy cold**, so she's staying at home today.

a bad cold

Valentina has an upset stomach and can't stop **throwing up**.

vomiting

I'm **in bad shape**. I was exhausted after running to catch the bus.

in poor physical condition

Uma is **up and about** following her operation last week.

able to walk around

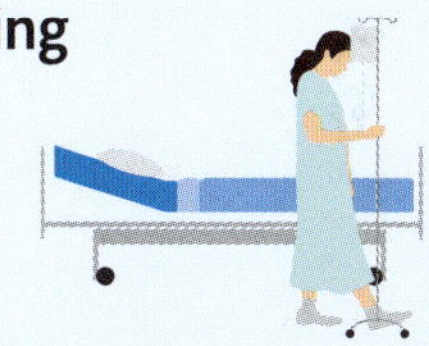

A week at a health spa was **just what the doctor ordered** after a stressful month at work.

exactly what was needed

A relaxing afternoon in the park helped me **recharge my batteries**.

regain my energy by resting

After a few days by the coast, Lauren began to feel **as right as rain**.

fit and healthy

Imran looks **the picture of health** since he started going to the gym.

extremely healthy

Aa 30.3 FILL IN THE GAPS, PUTTING THE WORDS IN THE CORRECT ORDER

road | on | the | recovery | to

Pablo is *on* *the* *road* *to* *recovery* after breaking his leg.

down | something | coming | with

1 I don't feel very well. I think I'm ______ ______ ______ ______ .

lease | life | on | new | a

2 Moving to the country has given Kira ______ ______ ______ ______ ______ .

of | a | clean | health | bill

3 Ollie received ______ ______ ______ ______ ______ from his doctor.

fiddle | fit | as | a | as

4 The dancers in this show have to be ______ ______ ______ ______ ______ .

30.4 LISTEN TO THE AUDIO AND MARK WHETHER THE SPEAKER IS TALKING ABOUT SICKNESS OR HEALTH

sickness ☐
health ☑

1 sickness ☐
health ☐

2 sickness ☐
health ☐

3 sickness ☐
health ☐

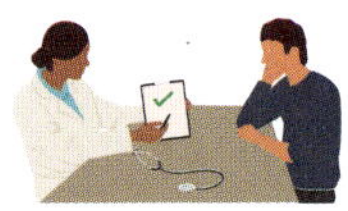

4 sickness ☐
health ☐

5 sickness ☐
health ☐

6 sickness ☐
health ☐

7 sickness ☐
health ☐

8 sickness ☐
health ☐

9 sickness ☐
health ☐

Aa 30.5 REWRITE THE SENTENCES, CORRECTING THE ERRORS

After a few days by the coast, Lauren began to feel **as good as rain**.
After a few days by the coast, Lauren began to feel as right as rain.

1. This music's far too loud! It has given me **a hitting headache**.

2. A week at a health spa was **just what the nurse ordered** after a stressful month at work.

3. Uma is **up and around** following her operation last week.

4. Imran looks **the drawing of health** since he started going to the gym.

5. A relaxing afternoon in the park helped me **load my batteries**.

Aa 30.6 WRITE THE CORRECT IDIOM NEXT TO ITS DEFINITION, FILLING IN THE MISSING LETTERS

not well, slightly sick or ill = *under the weather*

1. tired or in a bad state = t _ _ w _ _ _ _ f _ _ w _ _ _
2. vomiting = t _ _ _ _ _ _ _ u _
3. getting better = o _ t _ _ m _ _ _
4. in poor physical condition = i _ b _ _ s _ _ _ _
5. suddenly get worse = f _ _ _ _ u _
6. a bad cold = a h _ _ _ _ c _ _ _
7. become fitter and healthier = g _ _ i _ s _ _ _ _

31 Knowledge and education

31.1 KNOWLEDGE, THINKING, AND LEARNING

Mary's an expert in ancient history. She really knows her stuff.

knows a lot about a subject

Peter's brushing up on his French before his vacation in Paris.

revising or improving knowledge about something

The professor's astrophysics lecture went over my head.

was impossible to understand

Andrea only started work here last week. She's still learning the ropes.

learning the basic skills for a job

I can show you around my city. I know it like the back of my hand.

know it extremely well

Vineetha loves modern art. She knows it inside out.

knows it extremely well

We both thought of buying Dan a camera for his birthday. Great minds think alike!

Intelligent people have the same ideas (said in a humorous way).

My client wanted a completely new design. I had to put on my thinking cap.

think seriously or creatively about a problem

I just can't make heads or tails of this map. (US)

can't understand at all

Sumiko gave her speech without notes. She had learned it by heart.

memorized it

31.2 SCHOOL, COLLEGE, AND TESTS

Brad thought he would pass the test easily, but he only scraped by.

passed a test with difficulty

Ian is such a bookworm. He loves reading.

someone who enjoys reading books

When Souad took her piano test, she passed with flying colors.

passed easily, or performed very well

Ben accused Stefan of being a copycat. Their artworks were very similar.

someone who copies another person's idea

Trent is a teacher's pet. He always offers to carry the teacher's bag.

someone who seeks approval from a person in authority

31.3 SCIENCE AND TECHNOLOGY

Dion's new laptop is light-years ahead of his old one.

much more advanced than

Roman has bought himself a state-of-the-art TV set.

very modern and up-to-date

These doctors have made a breakthrough in their medical research.

an important discovery or achievement

Our cutting-edge products have made our company millions of dollars.

extremely modern and innovative

Ping's design for the new library really breaks the mold.

changes the usual way things are done

31.4 MATCH THE BEGINNINGS OF THE STATEMENTS TO THE CORRECT ENDINGS

Sumiko gave her speech without notes. → She had learned it by heart.

1. Brad thought he would pass the test easily,
2. Our cutting-edge products
3. The professor's astrophysics lecture
4. Ian is such a bookworm.
5. Vineetha loves modern art.
6. Ping's design for the new library
7. These doctors have made

- went over my head.
- have made our company millions of dollars.
- She had learned it by heart.
- She knows it inside out.
- but he only scraped by.
- a breakthrough in their medical research.
- He loves reading.
- really breaks the mold.

31.5 LISTEN TO THE AUDIO AND COMPLETE THE SENTENCES THAT DESCRIBE EACH PICTURE

Peter's *brushing up on* his French before his vacation in Paris.

1. We both thought of buying Dan a camera for his birthday. ______________________

2. Dion's new laptop is ______________________ his old one.

3. Ben accused Stefan of being ______________________. Their artworks were very similar.

4. Mary's an expert in ancient history. She really ______________________.

5. The professor's astrophysics lecture ______________________.

Aa 31.6 CROSS OUT THE INCORRECT WORDS IN EACH SENTENCE

Trent is a teacher's ~~friend~~ / **pet** / ~~help~~. He always offers to carry the teacher's bag.

1 
Andrea only started work here last week. She's still learning the **ropes** / **strings** / **lines**.

2 
I can show you around my city. I know it like the **back** / **palm** / **front** of my hand.

3 
My client wanted a completely new design. I had to put on my thinking **hat** / **cap** / **head**.

4 
I just can't make heads or **feet** / **bodies** / **tails** of this map.

5 
Peter's **brushing** / **sweeping** / **cleaning** up on his French before his vacation in Paris.

Aa 31.7 WRITE THE CORRECT IDIOM NEXT TO ITS DEFINITION

was impossible to understand	=	*went over my head*
1 passed a test with difficulty	=	
2 very modern and up-to-date	=	
3 someone who copies another person's idea	=	
4 someone who enjoys reading books	=	
5 can't understand at all	=	
6 an important discovery or achievement	=	
7 passed easily, or performed very well	=	

32 Money

32.1 IDIOMS ABOUT MONEY

Luisa had to pay **a hefty sum** to get a ticket for the game today.

a large amount of money

My uncle started his own business a few years ago, and now he's really **well off**.

comfortably rich

Marco had to **tighten his belt**, so he started bringing his own lunch to work.

spend less money

Sarah had to **pay through the nose** to get a taxi home after she missed the last train.

pay a lot of money

Luna wants to buy a house soon, so she's building up **a nest-egg**.

a large sum of money saved for a specific purpose

Donna **struck it rich** when she won the lottery.

suddenly became rich

Irena's new handbag was very **pricey**. It cost hundreds of dollars.

expensive

Aranza and Dominic decided to **go Dutch** at the end of the meal.

share the cost of a meal out equally

The shoes at the market **cost next to nothing**, so Jeremy bought three pairs.

were very cheap

If you don't turn off the lights when you leave the house, you're **throwing money down the drain**.

wasting money

I found it hard to make ends meet when I was a student, so I started working in a café.

pay for my basic needs

The popcorn in this movie theater is a rip-off! I prefer to bring my own snacks.

far more expensive than it should be

I loved looking after Nadia's cat while she was on vacation. It was easy money.

money earned for doing very little work

It was really generous of Imran to buy us dinner at that expensive restaurant, but he does like to throw money around.

show off by spending money

We ended up out of pocket when no one wanted to buy our ice cream.

with less money than we started with

Getting the car fixed will be expensive, but luckily I have saved for a rainy day.

saved money for when it might be needed unexpectedly

Mike is rolling in it. He's just bought himself another yacht.

extremely rich

The stall is closing in an hour, so it's selling its sandwiches at rock-bottom prices.

very low prices

My daughter wants a new smartphone. I keep telling her money doesn't grow on trees!

there is only a limited amount of money

Vegetables don't have to be expensive. Carrots and cabbage are dirt cheap at this store.

extremely cheap

32.2 MATCH THE PICTURES TO THE CORRECT SENTENCES

1 

2 

3 

4 

I loved looking after Nadia's cat while she was on vacation. It was easy money.

If you don't turn off the lights when you leave the house, you're throwing money down the drain.

My daughter wants a new smartphone. I keep telling her money doesn't grow on trees!

It was really generous of Imran to buy us dinner at that expensive restaurant, but he does like to throw money around.

Vegetables don't have to be expensive. Carrots and cabbage are dirt cheap at this store.

32.3 WRITE THE IDIOMS FROM THE PANEL IN THE CORRECT GROUPS

CHEAP	EXPENSIVE
dirt cheap	

pricey ~~dirt cheap~~ rock-bottom prices a hefty sum cost next to nothing a rip-off

32.4 MATCH THE BEGINNINGS OF THE IDIOMS TO THE CORRECT ENDINGS

money doesn't → grow on trees

1 tighten

2 saved for

3 out of

4 struck it

5 rolling

a rainy day

rich

grow on trees

his belt

in it

pocket

32.5 LISTEN TO THE AUDIO, THEN NUMBER THE SENTENCES IN THE ORDER YOU HEAR THEM

A. If you don't turn off the lights when you leave the house, you're throwing money down the drain. ☐

B. Sarah had to pay through the nose to get a taxi home after she missed the last train. ☐

C. My uncle started his own business a few years ago, and now he's really well off. [1]

D. The stall is closing in an hour, so it's selling its sandwiches at rock-bottom prices. ☐

E. My daughter wants a new smartphone. I keep telling her money doesn't grow on trees! ☐

F. Luisa had to pay a hefty sum to get a ticket for the game today. ☐

32.6 LOOK AT THE PICTURES AND COMPLETE THE SENTENCES

It was really generous of Imran to buy us dinner at that expensive restaurant, but he does like to *throw money around*.

1. I found it hard to ______________________ when I was a student, so I started working in a café.

2. Aranza and Dominic decided to ______________ at the end of the meal.

3. Luna wants to buy a house soon, so she's building up ______________________.

4. Marco had to ______________________, so he started bringing his own lunch to work.

5. Getting the car fixed will be expensive, but luckily I have ______________________.

33 Shopping

33.1 IDIOMS AND EXPRESSIONS ABOUT SHOPPING

I like to shop around before I buy a new sofa.

compare prices at various stores

Be careful, Max! That vase cost a fortune.

cost a lot of money

Tourists usually pay over the odds when they buy souvenirs. (UK)

pay more than is typical

My new suit cost an arm and a leg. I bought it from a tailor in Milan.

cost a large amount of money

Adrian loves to go bargain-hunting at his local market.

search for goods that are cheaper than normal

Martina found a designer jacket for a steal at a thrift store.

a very low price or good bargain

Most customers prefer to buy off-the-shelf products because they are cheaper.

mass-produced, commercially available

During the sales, many stores slash prices by more than 50 percent.

reduce prices dramatically

A valuable painting went under the hammer and sold for £3 million last week. (UK)

was sold at an auction

Javier drove a hard bargain, refusing to drop the price of his house.

was a tough negotiator

The taxi from the airport cost more than $70. It was highway robbery! (US)

far more expensive than it should have been

For her 50th birthday, Davina decided to splurge on a new sports car.

spend money extravagantly

After winning the lottery, Tomás went on a shopping spree.

bought a large number of things

This store sells designer labels at bargain-basement prices.

very low prices

Ayesha goes window shopping with her friends every Saturday.

looks at goods in store windows without buying them

Hannah needed a new party dress and found a good deal online.

a good price

On the last day of the sales, Sam and Hiromi shopped till they dropped.

did a lot of shopping

Austin needed some retail therapy, so he spent the afternoon at the mall.

shopping as a way of getting rid of stress

It was so quiet on Monday that we decided to close up shop for the afternoon. (US)

close a business temporarily or permanently

We were on a tight budget for our vacation, so we stayed in a cheap hostel.

had a small amount of money to spend

33.2 WRITE THE IDIOMS FROM THE PANEL IN THE CORRECT GROUPS

CHEAP	EXPENSIVE
a good deal	

highway robbery
~~a good deal~~
bargain-basement prices
cost an arm and a leg
pay over the odds
slash prices

33.3 LISTEN TO THE AUDIO, THEN NUMBER THE PICTURES IN THE ORDER YOU HEAR THEM

A ☐

B ☐

C ☐

D ☐

E 1

F ☐

G ☐

H ☐

I ☐

33.4 READ THE STATEMENTS AND MARK THE CORRECT MEANING

Tourists usually pay over the odds when they buy souvenirs.

They pay too much. ☑
They pay the right amount. ☐
They don't pay enough. ☐

1. Adrian loves to go bargain-hunting at his local market.

He looks for expensive things. ☐
He doesn't care what things cost. ☐
He looks for cheap things. ☐

2. Martina found a designer jacket for a steal at a thrift store.

She stole the jacket. ☐
The jacket was cheap. ☐
The jacket was expensive. ☐

3. During the sales, many stores slash prices by more than 50 percent.

They increase prices. ☐
They reduce prices a bit. ☐
They reduce prices a lot. ☐

4. Ayesha goes window shopping with her friends every Saturday.

Ayesha buys things. ☐
Ayesha doesn't buy anything. ☐
Ayesha buys windows. ☐

5. On the last day of the sales, Sam and Hiromi shopped till they dropped.

They bought lots of things. ☐
They didn't buy much. ☐
They fell over. ☐

Aa 33.5 MARK THE SENTENCES THAT ARE CORRECT

We were on a short budget for our vacation, so we stayed in a cheap hostel. ☐
We were on a tight budget for our vacation, so we stayed in a cheap hostel. ☑

1 

My new suit cost an arm and a leg. I bought it from a tailor in Milan. ☐
My new suit cost a hand and a foot. I bought it from a tailor in Milan. ☐

2 

After winning the lottery, Tomás went on a shopping ride. ☐
After winning the lottery, Tomás went on a shopping spree. ☐

3 

The taxi from the airport cost more than $70. It was highway robbery! ☐
The taxi from the airport cost more than $70. It was highway stealing! ☐

4 

Austin needed some retail therapy, so he spent the afternoon at the mall. ☐
Austin needed some shopping therapy, so he spent the afternoon at the mall. ☐

5 

This store sells designer labels at bargain-attic prices. ☐
This store sells designer labels at bargain-basement prices. ☐

6 

Javier ran a hard bargain, refusing to drop the price of his house. ☐
Javier drove a hard bargain, refusing to drop the price of his house. ☐

Aa 33.6 WRITE THE CORRECT IDIOM NEXT TO ITS DEFINITION, FILLING IN THE MISSING LETTERS

close a business temporarily or permanently = close up shop

1 spend money extravagantly = s _ _ _ _ _ _

2 compare prices at various stores = s _ _ _ a _ _ _ _ _

3 pay more than is typical = p _ _ o _ _ _ t _ _ o _ _ _

4 reduce prices dramatically = s _ _ _ _ p _ _ _ _ _

5 cost a lot of money = c _ _ _ a f _ _ _ _ _ _

34 Time

34.1 IDIOMS AND EXPRESSIONS ABOUT TIME

Júlio took his time finishing his painting. He wanted it to be perfect.

took the necessary time; didn't rush

Time's up! I need you to give me an answer now.

You have no more time to complete a task.

Victoria is always on time for her English class.

punctual

Huan only cooks at home once in a blue moon.

very rarely

You'll have to wait until the cows come home before Yuri fixes your car.

an extremely long time

That meeting really dragged on. Colm was almost asleep by the end.

lasted far too long

The teacher told Cory to stop wasting time on his phone.

spending time in an unproductive way

We must get a move on or we'll miss the start of the play.

hurry up

Driving to work during rush hour is such a drag. The traffic's terrible!

a boring experience that passes very slowly

It's been ages since I last went to the circus. I haven't been since I was a child.

a very long time

Today has flown by, and I still have so much work to do!

passed very quickly or too quickly

It's nearly midnight. It's about time we went home.

past the appropriate time

Finley's growing up so quickly! He was walking before we knew it.

unexpectedly soon or quickly

We arrived in the nick of time. The train was about to leave.

at the last possible moment

Our flight was delayed for a few hours, so we killed time playing cards.

kept busy while waiting

34.2 PARTS OF THE DAY

We were up at the crack of dawn to catch our flight.

extremely early in the morning

Ren arrived bright and early for his first day at work.

early in the morning

I was woken in the dead of night by a loud noise outside.

the middle of the night; the quietest part of the night

I worked on my assignment from dusk till dawn.

through the whole night

Fred stayed up until the wee hours, chatting with his grandfather.

very late at night

34.3 MATCH THE BEGINNINGS OF THE IDIOMS TO THE CORRECT ENDINGS

	in the nick → of time	move on
1	get a	blue moon
2	from dusk	of time
3	once in a	till dawn
4	before we	of dawn
5	at the crack	knew it

34.4 LISTEN TO THE AUDIO AND MARK THE IDIOMS YOU HEAR

- A a drag ☐
- B at the crack of dawn ☑
- C bright and early ☐
- D dragged on ☐
- E ages ☐
- F flown by ☐
- G killed time ☐
- H the dead of night ☐

34.5 CROSS OUT THE INCORRECT WORDS IN EACH SENTENCE

You'll have to wait until the ~~sheep~~ / ~~pigs~~ / cows come home before Yuri fixes your car.

1 
Time's out / up / off! I need you to give me an answer now.

2 
The teacher told Cory to stop wasting / losing / using time on his phone.

3 
I was woken in the death / die / dead of night by a loud noise outside.

4 
We were up at the split / crack / gap of dawn to catch our flight.

5 
That meeting really slowed / crawled / dragged on. Colm was almost asleep by the end.

Aa 34.6 MATCH THE DEFINITIONS TO THE CORRECT IDIOMS

kept busy while waiting → killed time

1. unexpectedly soon or quickly
2. very late at night
3. You have no more time to complete a task.
4. a boring experience that passes very slowly
5. at the last possible moment
6. passed very quickly or too quickly

- Time's up!
- before we knew it
- killed time
- a drag
- the wee hours
- flown by
- in the nick of time

Aa 34.7 LOOK AT THE PICTURES AND COMPLETE THE SENTENCES

We must *get a move on* or we'll miss the start of the play.

3. Ren arrived ________________ for his first day at work.

1. Júlio ________________ finishing his painting. He wanted it to be perfect.

4. It's nearly midnight. It's ________________ we went home.

2. Victoria is always ________________ for her English class.

5. Huan only cooks at home ________________ ________________.

35 Clothes

35.1 IDIOMS USING VOCABULARY ABOUT CLOTHES

When Juan won the national art prize, it was a feather in his cap.

an achievement to be proud of

Pedro's upset about failing the test. You'll have to handle him with kid gloves.

treat him very carefully or sensitively

If Sven wins the race, I'll eat my hat!

I'll be amazed (but I doubt it will happen)

I take my hat off to Jo for collecting so much money for charity this year.

I am very impressed with

My daughter thinks my taste in music is really old hat.

old-fashioned

My boss got very hot under the collar when I handed my report in late.

agitated and angry

The movie was a spy thriller with lots of cloak-and-dagger action.

involving mystery, spying, or things that happen in secret

Our plan to improve sales didn't work, but I have a new plan up my sleeve.

ready, but not yet common knowledge

Jane has a bee in her bonnet about people dropping litter on the sidewalk.

gets very angry and annoyed

Ian's become too big for his boots since his promotion. He always ignores me. (UK)

arrogant or self-important

We need to roll up our sleeves if we're going to finish painting the house today.

get ready to work hard

Cathy had been lining her pockets with company funds for years before the boss caught her.

making money illegally, often by corruption

Austin is in a lot of trouble. I wouldn't want to be in his shoes.

in his situation

This steak really is as tough as shoe leather. I need a sharper knife! (US)

difficult to cut or chew

If Gavin doesn't start working harder, we'll have to give him the boot.

force him to leave his job

My teacher explained that I would fail the exam if I didn't pull my socks up. (UK)

start working harder

My cousin is very emotional. He'll start an argument at the drop of a hat.

immediately, or without thinking too much about it

Carter is such a clever clogs. He's always the first to raise his hand in class. (UK)

a person who likes to show how intelligent they are

I don't think he thought about what he was saying. It was just an off-the-cuff comment.

unprepared and spontaneous

After working at the bank for 30 years, it was time for me to hang up my boots.

retire

Aa 35.2 MATCH THE BEGINNINGS OF THE SENTENCES TO THE CORRECT ENDINGS

I take my hat off to Jo → for collecting so much money for charity this year.

1. We need to roll up our sleeves
2. If Gavin doesn't start working harder,
3. Austin is in a lot of trouble.
4. My boss got very hot under the collar
5. The movie was a spy thriller
6. If Sven wins the race,
7. My daughter thinks my taste
8. Jane has a bee in her bonnet

- we'll have to give him the boot.
- when I handed my report in late.
- for collecting so much money for charity this year.
- if we're going to finish painting the house today.
- I wouldn't want to be in his shoes.
- about people dropping litter on the sidewalk.
- in music is really old hat.
- I'll eat my hat!
- with lots of cloak-and-dagger action.

Aa 35.3 REWRITE THE SENTENCES, CORRECTING THE ERRORS

I don't think he thought about what he was saying. It was just an **off-the-sleeve** comment.

I don't think he thought about what he was saying. It was just an off-the-cuff comment.

1. Pedro's upset about failing the test. You'll have to **handle him with kid socks**.

2. Ian's become **too big for his shoes** since his promotion. He always ignores me.

3. When Juan won the national art prize, it was **a feather in his hat**.

4. My teacher explained that I would fail the exam if I didn't **pull my shoes up**.

35.4 LISTEN TO THE AUDIO AND COMPLETE THE SENTENCES THAT DESCRIBE EACH PICTURE

Jane *has a bee in her bonnet* about people dropping litter on the sidewalk.

1 

This steak really is ______________ ______________. I need a sharper knife!

2 

My cousin is very emotional. He'll start an argument ______________ ______________.

3 

Carter is such ______________ ______________. He's always the first to raise his hand in class.

4 

After working at the bank for 30 years, it was time for me to ______________.

5 

We need to ______________ ______________ if we're going to finish painting the house today.

35.5 WRITE THE CORRECT IDIOM NEXT TO ITS DEFINITION, FILLING IN THE MISSING LETTERS

start working harder = p *u l l* m *y* s *o c k s* u *p*

1 force him to leave his job = g _ _ _ h _ _ t _ _ b _ _ _

2 ready, but not yet common knowledge = u _ m _ s _ _ _ _ _

3 in his situation = i _ h _ _ s _ _ _ _

4 get ready to work hard = r _ _ _ u _ o _ _ s _ _ _ _ _ _

5 retire = h _ _ _ u _ m _ b _ _ _ _

6 unprepared and spontaneous = o _ _ - t _ _ - c _ _ _

7 making money illegally = l _ _ _ _ _ h _ _ p _ _ _ _ _ _

8 old-fashioned = o _ _ h _ _

36 Working and relaxing

36.1 WORKING HARD

Nicole's **burning the candle at both ends**. She must be exhausted.

working very hard, from the early morning until late at night

I'm sorry, I can't talk to you for long. I **have my hands full**.

am very busy

Leo always **goes the extra mile** to keep our customers happy.

makes more of an effort than expected

It took a lot of **elbow grease** to get the old car looking good again.

hard work or cleaning

The police **left no stone unturned** in their efforts to solve the crime.

did everything possible to solve a problem

Samira was **snowed under** with complaints from unhappy customers.

extremely busy, or overwhelmed

Although Julie had never tried roller-skating before, she **gave it her best shot**.

tried her best

Adele's parents **pulled out all the stops** to make sure she had a wonderful 18th birthday.

did everything possible to succeed

Celia had to **put her head down** and finish her essay to meet the deadline. (US)

concentrate and work hard

We'll have to **roll up our sleeves** if we're going to finish the building this month.

be ready to work very hard

36.2 RELAXING

Akash usually takes 40 winks after he's finished his lunch.

has a short sleep

Kelly took a cat nap in the afternoon sun.

had a short sleep

After a long day working at the store, Marc likes to put his feet up and watch TV.

have a rest

We stopped to take a breather before loading the rest of the boxes into the van.

have a short break and a rest

We were up late at our housewarming party last night, so we're taking it easy today.

resting and relaxing

36.3 BEING LAZY

If you cut corners to save time, the quality of your work will suffer.

try to do things quickly and cheaply without thinking of quality

Carmen is not pulling her weight. I found her asleep at her desk again!

not working as hard as other members of the team

Erik was so lazy. He didn't lift a finger to help us clean up after the party.

did absolutely nothing

Brandon is a slacker. He looks at his phone all day and ignores the customers.

a very lazy person

I was such a lazybones when I was a student. I spent most of the time playing video games.

a lazy person

36.4 LISTEN TO THE AUDIO AND MARK THE CORRECT PICTURE FOR EACH SENTENCE YOU HEAR

Ⓐ ☐

Ⓑ ☐

Ⓒ ☑

1

Ⓐ ☐

Ⓑ ☐

Ⓒ ☐

2

Ⓐ ☐

Ⓑ ☐

Ⓒ ☐

3

Ⓐ ☐

Ⓑ ☐

Ⓒ ☐

4

Ⓐ ☐

Ⓑ ☐

Ⓒ ☐

5

Ⓐ ☐

Ⓑ ☐

Ⓒ ☐

36.5 READ THE STATEMENTS AND MARK THE CORRECT MEANING

Kelly took a cat nap in the afternoon sun.

Kelly worked hard. ☐
Kelly had a short sleep. ☑
Kelly has a cat. ☐

1. Nicole's burning the candle at both ends. She must be exhausted.

She's working hard. ☐
She's lazy. ☐
She has burned herself. ☐

2. We stopped to take a breather before loading the rest of the boxes into the van.

We slept. ☐
We had a drink. ☐
We rested. ☐

3. Although Julie had never tried roller-skating before, she gave it her best shot.

Julie won the competition. ☐
Julie tried her best. ☐
Julie lost the competition. ☐

4. Carmen is not pulling her weight. I found her asleep at her desk again!

Carmen is sick. ☐
Carmen is on a diet. ☐
Carmen is not working hard. ☐

5. It took a lot of elbow grease to get the old car looking good again.

It was hard work. ☐
It needed a lot of polish. ☐
It was easy. ☐

Aa 36.6 MARK THE SENTENCES THAT ARE CORRECT

We were up late at our housewarming party last night, so we're taking it simple today. ☐
We were up late at our housewarming party last night, so we're taking it easy today. ☑

1 

Leo always runs the extra mile to keep our customers happy. ☐
Leo always goes the extra mile to keep our customers happy. ☐

2 

Akash usually takes 40 blinks after he's finished his lunch. ☐
Akash usually takes 40 winks after he's finished his lunch. ☐

3 

I'm sorry, I can't talk to you for long. I have my hands full. ☐
I'm sorry, I can't talk to you for long. I have my arms full. ☐

4 

Celia had to put her head down and finish her essay to meet the deadline. ☐
Celia had to put her face down and finish her essay to meet the deadline. ☐

5 

Brandon is a relaxer. He looks at his phone all day and ignores the customers. ☐
Brandon is a slacker. He looks at his phone all day and ignores the customers. ☐

6 

After a long day working at the store, Marc likes to put his legs up and watch TV. ☐
After a long day working at the store, Marc likes to put his feet up and watch TV. ☐

Aa 36.7 WRITE THE CORRECT IDIOM NEXT TO ITS DEFINITION

makes more of an effort than expected = *goes the extra mile*

1. did everything possible to succeed = ______________________
2. be ready to work very hard = ______________________
3. extremely busy, or overwhelmed = ______________________
4. hard work or cleaning = ______________________
5. did absolutely nothing = ______________________

37 Movement and progress

37.1 IDIOMS ABOUT MOVEMENT AND PROGRESS

The traffic usually moves at a snail's pace during the rush hour.

extremely slowly

The hikers forged ahead in spite of the terrible snowstorm.

made good progress

The children threw the ball back and forth as they played outside.

in one direction, then back again

Astronauts made great strides in space exploration in the 1960s.

made a lot of progress

The guests made a beeline for all the cakes on the table.

moved quickly and in a straight line toward

Marion is going to up sticks and move to Bristol. (UK)

take her belongings and move somewhere else

I've been at my desk all day. I'm going to stretch my legs and make some coffee.

go for a short walk after sitting down for a long time

I want to buy a house this year, so I've set the wheels in motion and arranged some viewings.

done something to start a process

Our company has blazed a trail with these new environmentally friendly cars.

done something that has never been done before

I was late for my business meeting, so I had to eat lunch on the run. (US)

while walking or traveling

Maisie's restaurant is up and running. The first diners arrived at lunchtime.

open and working well

I'm running around like a headless chicken trying to get the meal ready for my guests tonight.

rushing around trying to do too many things at once

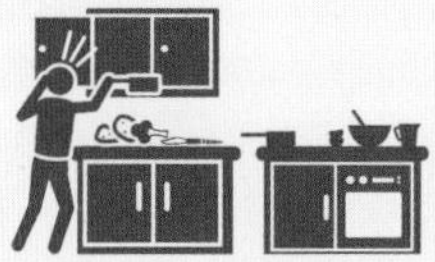

Scientists are on the verge of developing intelligent robots.

very close to doing something

Slowly but surely, my daughter is learning to ride a bike.

slowly, but at a steady rate of progress

Julia used to be so disorganized, but has really got her act together recently.

started to behave in a more organized and serious way

After squeezing our luggage into the car, we were ready to hit the road.

begin a trip or a drive

I've been going around in circles trying to write this report, but I haven't been given enough information.

not making any progress

After losing a few games earlier this month, the team is back on track now.

working well again after experiencing problems

The client hates my design for the company logo, so it's back to the drawing board.

I have to start again or try another idea

We had just finished repairing the road and now it has been damaged in a storm. It's back to square one.

back to the beginning

Aa 37.2 REWRITE THE SENTENCES, PUTTING THE WORDS IN THE CORRECT ORDER

her | together | act | got

Julia used to be so disorganized, but has really *got her act together* recently.

to | board | drawing | back | it's | the

1. The client hates my design for the company logo, so ______ ______ ______ ______ ______ ______ .

pace | snail's | a | at

2. The traffic usually moves ______ ______ ______ ______ during the rush hour.

a | for | made | beeline

3. The guests ______ ______ ______ ______ all the cakes on the table.

verge | on | of | the

4. Scientists are ______ ______ ______ ______ developing intelligent robots.

37.3 LISTEN TO THE AUDIO, THEN NUMBER THE SENTENCES IN THE ORDER YOU HEAR THEM

A. I've been at my desk all day. I'm going to stretch my legs and make some coffee. ☐

B. Our company has blazed a trail with these new environmentally friendly cars. ☐

C. I want to buy a house this year, so I've set the wheels in motion and arranged some viewings. *1*

D. After losing a few games earlier this month, the team is back on track now. ☐

E. Marion is going to up sticks and move to Bristol. ☐

Aa 37.4 MATCH THE IDIOMS TO THE CORRECT DEFINITIONS

	back and forth → in one direction, then back again	begin a trip or a drive
1	hit the road	not making any progress
2	up and running	in one direction, then back again
3	back to square one	made a lot of progess
4	going around in circles	open and working well
5	made great strides	back to the beginning

Aa 37.5 LOOK AT THE PICTURES AND COMPLETE THE SENTENCES

I've been at my desk all day. I'm going to *stretch my legs* and make some coffee.

3 ______________________________, my daughter is learning to ride a bike.

1 The hikers ______________________________ in spite of the terrible snowstorm.

4 I was late for my business meeting, so I had to eat lunch ______________________________.

2 I'm ______________________________ trying to get the meal ready for my guests tonight.

5 The children threw the ball ______________________________ ______________________________ as they played outside.

38 Rules, law, and authority

38.1 IDIOMS AND EXPRESSIONS ABOUT RULES AND THE LAW

It's important to obey the law when you're cycling in the city.

follow the commands of the law

Ben suffered the consequences of his misbehavior and had to wash the car.

was punished for something

Gavin broke the law when he drove through a red light.

disobeyed the law

Since leaving jail, Crystal has kept on the straight and narrow.

stayed out of trouble

Danielle decided to bend the rules and let her kids stay up later than usual.

relax the rules a little

It was the first time Raul had been caught speeding, so the police let him off the hook.

chose not to punish him

38.2 IDIOMS USING VOCABULARY ABOUT THE BODY

We have a meeting with the head of our department every week.

the person with the most authority

Seth took the law into his own hands and confronted the vandals.

dealt with crime without using the legal system

Carla refused to toe the line and wear the same uniform as the other students.

follow or conform to the rules

Despite being rude to a customer, Ed only received a slap on the wrist, and got a verbal warning.

a minor punishment

It's the children who **rule the roost** in Kaylee's family. They don't respect her.

have control

It was the **day of reckoning**. The judge was about to sentence Mason for burglary.

day when someone finds out the consequences of their actions

The vandals **got their just deserts** and had to do community service.

received the punishment they deserved

The jury discussed the evidence and **reached a verdict** after two days.

decided whether someone was guilty or innocent

Paul has really **crossed the line** this time. He's eaten all his sister's birthday cake.

behaved in a very inappropriate way

Chrissie **calls the shots** in our restaurant. She decides what's on the menu.

has the authority or power

Pedro's father **put his foot down** and refused to let him watch TV.

made a firm decision

Leah's manager **twisted her arm**, and she agreed to work late.

put pressure on her

The party **got out of hand**, so the neighbors called the police.

became impossible to control

Jack's boss is always **breathing down his neck**. He wants more independence.

watching or supervising him too closely

38.3 LISTEN TO THE AUDIO AND MARK THE IDIOMS YOU HEAR

	let him off the hook ☑	rule the roost ☐	put his foot down ☐
1	crossed the line ☐	a slap on the wrist ☐	calls the shots ☐
2	got out of hand ☐	bend the rules ☐	broke the law ☐
3	toe the line ☐	obey the law ☐	twisted her arm ☐
4	reached a verdict ☐	broke the law ☐	suffered the consequences ☐
5	got their just deserts ☐	calls the shots ☐	crossed the line ☐

Aa 38.4 MATCH THE PICTURES TO THE CORRECT SENTENCES

1 

2 

3 

4 

5 

It's the children who rule the roost in Kaylee's family. They don't respect her.

Paul has really crossed the line this time. He's eaten all his sister's birthday cake.

It was the day of reckoning. The judge was about to sentence Mason for burglary.

Seth took the law into his own hands and confronted the vandals.

It's important to obey the law when you're cycling in the city.

Ben suffered the consequences of his misbehavior and had to wash the car.

Aa 38.5 REWRITE THE SENTENCES, CORRECTING THE ERRORS

Danielle decided to **twist the rules** and let her kids stay up later than usual.
Danielle decided to bend the rules and let her kids stay up later than usual.

1. Carla refused to **walk the line** and wear the same uniform as the other students.

2. Jack's boss is always **breathing down his ear**. He wants more independence.

3. The party **got out of reach**, so the neighbors called the police.

4. Since leaving jail, Crystal has **kept on the strict and narrow**.

5. Pedro's father **put his leg down** and refused to let him watch TV.

Aa 38.6 WRITE THE CORRECT IDIOM NEXT TO ITS DEFINITION

received the punishment they deserved	=	*got their just deserts*
1 chose not to punish him	=	
2 decided whether someone was guilty or innocent	=	
3 put pressure on her	=	
4 the person with the most authority	=	
5 has the authority or power	=	
6 a minor punishment	=	

39 Success and failure

39.1 SUCCESS

Melissa did really well in the race. She won it hands down.

won it easily and with little effort

Nathan's first book was an overnight success. It sold a million copies in a month.

successful very quickly

Jane really nailed it with her jokes. The audience loved her.

was successful, popular, or accurate

Miguel has hit the jackpot with his new ice cream machine.

become financially successful

Malik's band has hit the big time. It performed at the national stadium last night.

become very successful

Tyler has finally reached the dizzy heights of head chef. He started out doing the dishes.

a very important position

39.2 FAILURE

Tim's beating a dead horse. Nobody wants to buy his old car. (US)

wasting energy on something that will never succeed

Margaret's performance fell flat on its face. She can't sing!

was a complete failure

The barbecue was an utter failure. It rained and none of my friends turned up.

a complete failure

The decorators have really screwed up this job! We won't use them again.

made a mess of

The dancers **brought the house down** with their fantastic performance.

greatly impressed an audience

The outdoor exhibition has been **a runaway success**. Lots of people have come to see it.

extremely successful

Lucy's beauty salon is **going from strength to strength**. She's opening another soon.

becoming increasingly successful

The soccer tournament **ran like clockwork**. Everyone really enjoyed it.

happened as planned, without any problems

I knew Helena would **go places** as an athlete. She was so good at running at school.

become successful

Erica's presentation **worked like a charm** with the investors. They loved the designs.

was very impressive

My dinner party started to **go sideways** when I spilled soup everywhere. (US)

go wrong, or fail

Nicola's decision to take her dog shopping turned out to be **a recipe for disaster**.

a cause of major problems

Kevin's career is **on the ropes**. His boss has given him an official warning.

going badly, or failing

The gang's plan to rob the bank **went belly up** when a policeman recognized Mike.

failed completely

Aa 39.3 WRITE THE IDIOMS FROM THE PANEL IN THE CORRECT GROUPS

SUCCESS	FAILURE
hit the big time	______________
______________	______________
______________	______________

on the ropes ~~hit thebig time~~ worked like a charm

go sideways screwed up brought the house down

Aa 39.4 LOOK AT THE PICTURES AND COMPLETE THE SENTENCES

Tim's *beating a dead horse*. Nobody wants to buy his old car.

1 The gang's plan to rob the bank ______________ ______________ when a policeman recognized Mike.

2 Nicola's decision to take her dog shopping turned out to be ______________.

3 Nathan's first book was ______________ ______________. It sold a million copies in a month.

4 Lucy's beauty salon is ______________ ______________. She's opening another soon.

5 Margaret's performance ______________ ______________. She can't sing!

39.5 LISTEN TO THE AUDIO AND MARK WHETHER THE SPEAKER IS TALKING ABOUT SUCCESS OR FAILURE

success ☑
failure ☐

1 success ☐
failure ☐

2 success ☐
failure ☐

3 success ☐
failure ☐

4 success ☐
failure ☐

5 success ☐
failure ☐

6 success ☐
failure ☐

7 success ☐
failure ☐

8 success ☐
failure ☐

9 success ☐
failure ☐

39.6 MATCH THE DEFINITIONS TO THE CORRECT IDIOMS

	was successful, popular, or accurate → nailed it	go sideways
1	won it easily and with little effort	brought the house down
2	go wrong, or fail	nailed it
3	successful very quickly	fell flat on its face
4	greatly impressed an audience	won it hands down
5	was a complete failure	a recipe for disaster
6	becoming increasingly successful	an overnight success
7	a cause of major problems	hit the jackpot
8	become financially successful	screwed up
9	made a mess of	going from strength to strength

40 Work and business 1

40.1 WORK AND BUSINESS IDIOMS

Carlos has lots of hands-on experience working with horses.

knowledge and skill gained through doing something

Our snack bars are delicious, healthy, and affordable. In a nutshell, your customers will love them.

in a few words

Rory goes the extra mile to make sure his customers are satisfied.

does more than is expected

I'm afraid Glen's busy. He's up to his eyeballs grading papers.

extremely busy

Irena's internship at the fashion firm helped her to get a foot in the door.

an opportunity to start doing a new job

Despite the snow, it's business as usual at the store today.

the normal routine of a company or workplace

I was fired from my job at the salon after I dyed a customer's hair green by mistake.

forced to leave a job

Andrew made sure he had his ducks in a row before his presentation.

had everything prepared and organized

Sara has handed in her notice at work. She's going to study engineering.

formally told her employer that she will leave her job

We offer customers a discount when they recommend us to a friend. It's a win-win situation.

a situation with a positive outcome for everyone

Victor is climbing the career ladder. He started work as a receptionist last year and he's already a manager.

getting higher pay and more responsibility at work

After studying for many years, Anna embarked on a career as a surgeon.

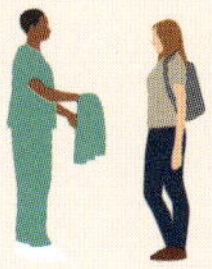

started a new career

Maya is a great designer. She always thinks outside the box.

thinks about things in an original way

We're working around the clock to make sure the new subway line opens on time.

working all day and night

I'm afraid Katya can't come to the phone. She's tied up in meetings all morning.

busy doing something else

40.2 EXPRESSIONS WITH "JOB"

I'm really bored at work, so I've decided to start job hunting.

looking for a new job

Working at the kindergarten is tiring, but the job satisfaction is high.

the pleasure you get from work

Miguel has just landed a job at a photography firm in San Francisco.

found a good job

I'm surprised Cheryl has managed to hold down a job at the store for so long. She's always being rude to customers.

keep a job

I used to work night shifts, but now I have a nine-to-five job.

a job with regular daytime hours, from Monday to Friday

Aa 40.3 FILL IN THE GAPS, PUTTING THE WORDS IN THE CORRECT ORDER

to | eyeballs | his | up

I'm afraid Glen's busy. He's _up_ _to_ _his_ _eyeballs_ grading papers.

ducks | a | had | row | his | in

1. Andrew made sure he ______ ______ ______ ______ ______ ______ before his presentation.

box | the | outside | thinks

2. Maya is a great designer. She always ______ ______ ______ ______ .

in | foot | a | door | the

3. Irena's internship at the fashion firm helped her to get ______ ______ ______ ______ ______ .

the | working | clock | around

4. We're ______ ______ ______ ______ to make sure the new subway line opens on time.

40.4 LISTEN TO THE AUDIO, THEN NUMBER THE PICTURES IN THE ORDER YOU HEAR THEM

A ☐

B ☐

C ☐

D ☐

E _1_

F ☐

G ☐

H ☐

Aa 40.5 CROSS OUT THE INCORRECT WORDS IN EACH SENTENCE

Despite the snow, it's business as ~~normal~~ / **usual** / ~~ever~~ at the store today.

1 Carlos has lots of **hands-on** / **head-on** / **hands-up** experience working with horses.

2 Sara has handed in her **letter** / **statement** / **notice** at work. She's going to study engineering.

3 After studying for many years, Anna embarked on a **job** / **career** / **work** as a surgeon.

4 I'm really bored at work, so I've decided to start job **looking** / **searching** / **hunting**.

5 Rory goes the extra **distance** / **mile** / **length** to make sure his customers are satisfied.

Aa 40.6 WRITE THE CORRECT IDIOM NEXT TO ITS DEFINITION, FILLING IN THE MISSING LETTERS

the pleasure you get from work = j o b s a t i s f a c t i o n

1 found a good job = l _ _ _ _ _ _ a j _ _

2 in a few words = i _ a n _ _ _ _ _ _ _

3 busy doing something else = t _ _ _ u _

4 does more than is expected = g _ _ _ t _ _ e _ _ _ _ m _ _ _

5 forced to leave a job = f _ _ _ _

41 Work and business 2

41.1 IDIOMS USING VOCABULARY ABOUT COLORS

There's a lot of red tape involved in health and safety in the warehouse.

administration, paperwork, or rules and regulations

We decided to blacklist this supplier after they sent us faulty products.

put on a list of untrustworthy people or organizations

My dad had a blue-collar job in the construction industry.

a job that involves manual or physical work

I have a white-collar job in an investment bank.

an office-based or administrative job

Our ski clothing stores are in the red because there hasn't been any snow this winter.

losing money, or in debt

Boris was given a golden handshake when he retired from the company. (UK)

a payment or gift from a company to someone who is leaving it

41.2 IDIOMS USING VOCABULARY ABOUT SPORTS

We've already reduced our price by 25 percent. The ball is in your court.

It is your turn to act.

Our boss is leaving the restaurant soon, and Angela is the front-runner to get his job.

the person or organization most likely to win something

We ask all our interview candidates the same questions to create a level playing field.

an environment in which everyone has equal opportunities

Emily is a team player. She works so well with all her colleagues at the bookstore.

a person who works well with other people

41.3 IDIOMS USING VOCABULARY ABOUT FOOD

Our new bags are **selling like hotcakes**. We need to order more.

selling quickly in large numbers

After many years in journalism, Simon became **a big cheese** in the media.

an important person in a company or industry

Evan is always asking me what to do. I feel like I have to **spoon-feed** him.

give too much help to

My gardening business is starting to **bring home the bacon**.

make money

I play in a band every weekend, but teaching guitar is my **bread and butter**.

main source of income

41.4 IDIOMS USING VOCABULARY ABOUT ANIMALS

I've decided to leave **the rat race** and move to the country.

a way of urban working life that puts people under pressure

Raul isn't our boss, but he still tries to be **the top dog** in our team. He's always telling us what to do.

the most important person

We made **the lion's share** of our profits last year from our new smartphone.

the largest part

Our range of cereal is **a cash cow**. It's cheap to make and customers love it.

a product or investment that gives you a steady income

My boss is **a fat cat**. He earns lots of money, but doesn't work very hard.

an overpaid and lazy person

Aa 41.5 MATCH THE BEGINNINGS OF THE SENTENCES TO THE CORRECT ENDINGS

I play in a band every weekend, → but teaching guitar is my bread and butter.

1. I've decided to leave the rat race
2. My dad had a blue-collar job
3. We decided to blacklist this supplier
4. After many years in journalism,
5. There's a lot of red tape involved

- after they sent us faulty products.
- in the construction industry.
- but teaching guitar is my bread and butter.
- and move to the country.
- in health and safety in the warehouse.
- Simon became a big cheese in the media.

41.6 LISTEN TO THE AUDIO AND COMPLETE THE SENTENCES THAT DESCRIBE EACH PICTURE

There's a lot of *red tape* involved in health and safety in the warehouse.

1 We ask all our interview candidates the same questions to create ________________ .

2 Our range of cereal is ________________ . It's cheap to make and customers love it.

3 I have ________________ in an investment bank.

4 Our new bags are ________________ ________________ . We need to order more.

5 Evan is always asking me what to do. I feel like I have to ________________ him.

Aa 41.7 REWRITE THE SENTENCES, CORRECTING THE ERRORS

My boss is **a lazy cat**. He earns lots of money, but doesn't work very hard.
My boss is a fat cat. He earns lots of money, but doesn't work very hard.

1. We ask all our interview candidates the same questions to create **an equal playing field**.

____

2. Emily is **a sporting player**. She works so well with all her colleagues at the bookstore.

____

3. Our boss is leaving the restaurant soon, and Angela is **the front-winner** to get his job.

____

4. We've already reduced our price by 25 percent. **The ball is in your field.**

____

5. I play in a band every weekend, but teaching guitar is **my bread and cheese**.

____

6. Boris was given **a silver handshake** when he retired from the company.

____

Aa 41.8 WRITE THE CORRECT IDIOM NEXT TO ITS DEFINITION

a person who works well with other people = *a team player*

1. losing money, or in debt = ______________________________
2. make money = ______________________________
3. the largest part = ______________________________
4. the most important person = ______________________________
5. an office-based or administrative job = ______________________________

42 Sports

42.1 IDIOMS USING VOCABULARY ABOUT SPORTS

The party was already in full swing when we arrived.

very busy and lively

I've failed my driving test for the tenth time. I think it's time to throw in the towel.

admit defeat, or stop trying to do something

Bruno has taken my parking space at work again. Right, the gloves are off!

an argument or competition will be very intense

Hiroto is really on the ball and never makes a mistake at work.

alert and efficient

Our client threw us a curveball when she said we'd have to cater for another 50 guests at her wedding.

did something surprising that was difficult to deal with

I often have to work evenings, but I knew the score when I decided to accept this job.

understood a situation, especially its disadvantages

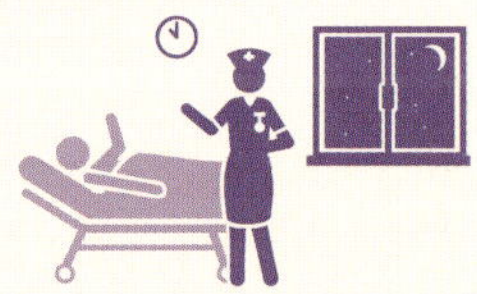

This client keeps moving the goalposts. Now she wants the bedroom painted red.

changing the desired end result

We don't have enough time to train our employees properly. They'll just have to sink or swim.

succeed by their own efforts, or fail

At this stage of the game, it's difficult to say how long it will take to fix your roof.

at this point in the process

I was having a difficult meeting with my boss, but was saved by the bell when he got called into another meeting.

rescued from a difficult situation at the last minute

I'm trying to start my own business, and cleared a hurdle today when the bank agreed to lend me money.

successfully dealt with a problem

Sleepless nights are par for the course when you have a baby.

to be expected

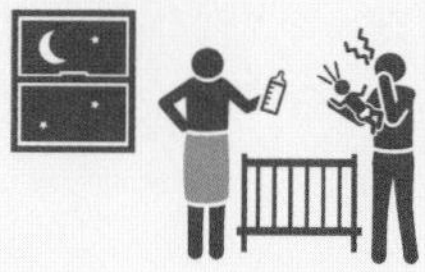

The service in this restaurant is really below par. We've been waiting for our food for an hour!

not to the expected standard

I'm sorry you didn't get through to the next round, Cameron. You win some, you lose some!

You can't succeed at everything.

The plumber gave us a ballpark figure for the cost of the new bathroom.

an estimate

I've had cats and rabbits before, but looking after a dog is a whole new ball game.

a completely different situation

We've got a lot of unpacking to do, so let's get the ball rolling.

start a process

The firefighters tackled the fire at the warehouse and made sure everyone got out safely.

dealt with

I was thrown in at the deep end when my colleague was sick and I had to run the café on my own on my first day.

put in an unexpected and difficult situation

All our gardeners are really hardworking, but Hannah is in a league of her own.

outstanding; exceptionally talented

Aa 42.2 MARK THE SENTENCES THAT ARE CORRECT

Sleepless nights are par for the field when you have a baby. ☐
Sleepless nights are par for the course when you have a baby. ☑

1. All our gardeners are really hardworking, but Hannah is in a league of her own. ☐
   All our gardeners are really hardworking, but Hannah is in a game of her own. ☐

2. This client keeps moving the net. Now she wants the bedroom painted red. ☐
   This client keeps moving the goalposts. Now she wants the bedroom painted red. ☐

3. We don't have enough time to train our employees properly. They'll just have to sink or float. ☐
   We don't have enough time to train our employees properly. They'll just have to sink or swim. ☐

4. We've got a lot of unpacking to do, so let's get the ball rolling. ☐
   We've got a lot of unpacking to do, so let's get the ball going. ☐

5. I often have to work evenings, but I knew the score when I decided to accept this job. ☐
   I often have to work evenings, but I knew the goal when I decided to accept this job. ☐

Aa 42.3 MATCH THE DEFINITIONS TO THE CORRECT IDIOMS

	changing the desired end result → moving the goalposts	a ballpark figure
1	successfully dealt with a problem	par for the course
2	very busy and lively	moving the goalposts
3	an estimate	in full swing
4	to be expected	cleared a hurdle
5	not to the expected standard	on the ball
6	alert and efficient	get the ball rolling
7	start a process	below par

42.4 LISTEN TO THE AUDIO AND MARK THE IDIOMS YOU HEAR

on the ball	☑	a whole new ball game	☐	get the ball rolling	☐
1 moving the goalposts	☐	the gloves are off	☐	in full swing	☐
2 at this stage of the game	☐	a whole new ball game	☐	sink or swim	☐
3 throw in the towel	☐	cleared a hurdle	☐	thrown in at the deep end	☐
4 saved by the bell	☐	a ballpark figure	☐	below par	☐
5 throw in the towel	☐	saved by the bell	☐	threw us a curveball	☐

42.5 LOOK AT THE PICTURES AND COMPLETE THE SENTENCES

The party was already *in full swing* when we arrived.

3 The plumber gave us ______________ for the cost of the new bathroom.

1 The firefighters ______________ the fire at the warehouse and made sure everyone got out safely.

4 I'm sorry you didn't get through to the next round, Cameron. ______________

2 I've had cats and rabbits before, but looking after a dog is ______________ .

5 I've failed my driving test for the tenth time. I think it's time to ______________ .

43 "Make" and "do"

43.1 EXPRESSIONS WITH "MAKE"

I **made some friends** from the local area while I was on vacation.

I was really pleased when Sue **made a cake** for my birthday.

These desserts all look so good! It's difficult to **make a choice**.

I **made a phone call** to our client in India to discuss some important business.

Doug is **making progress** on his new novel and hopes to finish it soon.

I was quite offended when Laura **made a joke** about my new sweater.

We're **making arrangements** for our summer vacation in Italy.

My daughter always **makes her bed** in the morning.

The children had fun painting, but they've really **made a mess**.

There's something wrong with the photocopier. It's **making a** strange **noise**.

43.2 EXPRESSIONS WITH "DO"

Luiz **does the cooking** every evening after he gets home from work.

Katy is **doing well** in her new job. She's getting lots of customers.

We **did an experiment** in the laboratory as part of our research project.

Do your best in the game today! I know you can beat the other team.

Paul and Liam **do the laundry** every Sunday so that they have clean clothes for work.

Can you **do me a favor** and get that book down from the shelf?

Zoe **did her hair** before her best friend's engagement party.

The flood **did** a lot of **damage** to our house, so we had to move out.

I always **do my homework** as soon as I get home from school.

I want to get fit, so I've started **doing exercise** every day.

Aa 43.3 CROSS OUT THE INCORRECT WORD IN EACH SENTENCE

These desserts all look so good! It's difficult to **make** / ~~do~~ a choice.

1. Doug is **making** / **doing** progress on his new novel and hopes to finish it soon.
2. I want to get fit, so I've started **making** / **doing** exercise every day.
3. **Make** / **Do** your best in the game today! I know you can beat the other team.
4. There's something wrong with the photocopier. It's **making** / **doing** a strange noise.
5. I always **make** / **do** my homework as soon as I get home from school.
6. The children had fun painting, but they've really **made** / **done** a mess.
7. Can you **make** / **do** me a favor and get that book down from the shelf?

Aa 43.4 MARK THE SENTENCES THAT ARE CORRECT

We're making arrangements for our summer vacation in Italy. ✓
We're doing arrangements for our summer vacation in Italy. ☐

1. 

Zoe made her hair before her best friend's engagement party. ☐
Zoe did her hair before her best friend's engagement party. ☐

2. 

I made a phone call to our client in India to discuss some important business. ☐
I did a phone call to our client in India to discuss some important business. ☐

3. 

I was quite offended when Laura made a joke about my new sweater. ☐
I was quite offended when Laura did a joke about my new sweater. ☐

4. 

The flood made a lot of damage to our house, so we had to move out. ☐
The flood did a lot of damage to our house, so we had to move out. ☐

5. 

We made an experiment in the laboratory as part of our research project. ☐
We did an experiment in the laboratory as part of our research project. ☐

43.5 LISTEN TO THE AUDIO, THEN NUMBER THE PICTURES IN THE ORDER YOU HEAR THEM

A ☐

B ☐

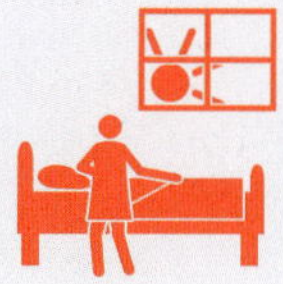
C 1

D ☐

E ☐

F ☐

G ☐

H ☐

43.6 FILL IN THE GAPS USING THE CORRECT FORM OF "MAKE" OR "DO"

Katy is *doing* well in her new job. She's getting lots of customers.

1. I __________ some friends from the local area while I was on vacation.
2. I always __________ my homework as soon as I get home from school.
3. We're __________ arrangements for our summer vacation in Italy.
4. I was really pleased when Sue __________ a cake for my birthday.
5. We __________ an experiment in the laboratory as part of our research project.
6. I was quite offended when Laura __________ a joke about my new sweater.
7. The flood __________ a lot of damage to our house, so we had to move out.
8. I want to get fit, so I've started __________ exercise every day.
9. My daughter always __________ her bed in the morning.
10. Can you __________ me a favor and get that book down from the shelf?

44 "Give" and "take"

44.1 EXPRESSIONS WITH "GIVE"

The interviewers asked me to give an example of my best work.

The professor gave a speech to the students about her new discovery.

I had a big suitcase, so Selma offered to give me a lift to the airport.

When Carole had her first baby, she chose to give birth in a hospital.

The dog gave the impression that he wanted to go out for a walk.

Drivers should always give priority to pedestrians.

Emily is giving a presentation about the company's sales figures.

My father gave me a hug when he heard I'd passed my final exam.

When Danny got to the hotel, he gave me a call to say he had arrived safely.

The journalist kept asking the politician to give an answer to the question.

44.2 EXPRESSIONS WITH "TAKE"

Jorge gets up very early, so he usually **takes a nap** after lunch.

Zora **took a bite** from her piece of birthday cake. It was delicious!

Hamid **took a photo** of his class in front of the Colosseum.

Dwayne likes to **take a shower** as soon as he gets home from work.

Near the end of the race, Axel passed the other athletes and **took the lead**.

Fiona asked us to **take a look** at her new motorcycle. She's really proud of it.

Mario and I are **taking a** drawing **class** this evening.

The receptionist asked me to **take a seat** while I waited for the hairdresser.

We decided to **take a chance** with the weather and set off on our hike.

Oscar had to **take a** fitness **test** before working as a police officer.

Aa 44.3 WRITE THE EXPRESSIONS FROM THE PANEL UNDER THE CORRECT VERBS

GIVE	TAKE
a presentation	

~~a presentation~~ an example a photo
a chance the impression a nap birth
a bite a shower a seat a speech priority
me a hug the lead an answer a look

Aa 44.4 MATCH THE PICTURES TO THE CORRECT SENTENCES

Dwayne likes to take a shower as soon as he gets home from work.

1 

Zora took a bite from her piece of birthday cake. It was delicious!

2 

Near the end of the race, Axel passed the other athletes and took the lead.

3 

Emily is giving a presentation about the company's sales figures.

4 

Hamid took a photo of his class in front of the Colosseum.

Aa 44.5 MATCH THE BEGINNINGS OF THE SENTENCES TO THE CORRECT ENDINGS

	Beginnings	Endings
	Dwayne likes to take a shower	that he wanted to go out for a walk.
1	I had a big suitcase, so Selma offered	a drawing class this evening.
2	The dog gave the impression	as soon as he gets home from work.
3	Mario and I are taking	to give me a lift to the airport.
4	The receptionist asked me to take	priority to pedestrians.
5	Drivers should always give	a seat while I waited for the hairdresser.

44.6 LISTEN TO THE AUDIO, THEN NUMBER THE SENTENCES IN THE ORDER YOU HEAR THEM

A Emily is giving a presentation about the company's sales figures. ☐

B Drivers should always give priority to pedestrians. [1]

C Jorge gets up very early, so he usually takes a nap after lunch. ☐

D My father gave me a hug when he heard I'd passed my final exam. ☐

E When Carole had her first baby, she chose to give birth in a hospital. ☐

F Oscar had to take a fitness test before working as a police officer. ☐

G The interviewers asked me to give an example of my best work. ☐

44.7 CROSS OUT THE INCORRECT WORD IN EACH SENTENCE

We decided to ~~give~~ / **take** a chance with the weather and set off on our hike.

1 
When Danny got to the hotel, he **gave** / **took** me a call to say he had arrived safely.

2 
Hamid **gave** / **took** a photo of his class in front of the Colosseum.

3 
The professor **gave** / **took** a speech to the students about her new discovery.

4 
Emily is **giving** / **taking** a presentation about the company's sales figures.

5 
Dwayne likes to **give** / **take** a shower as soon as he gets home from work.

45 "Have" and "get"

45.1 EXPRESSIONS WITH "HAVE"

Shreya's going to have a baby this summer.

Colin has a cold. He's staying at home today.

Lily had a conversation with another passenger on the train.

Tiffany had fun at the festival with her friends.

After gardening all morning, we were so tired that we needed to have a rest.

Michael and Heather had an argument about the rules of the game.

Sadiq has lunch in the park when the weather's nice.

I have an appointment to see the vet at 2 o'clock this afternoon.

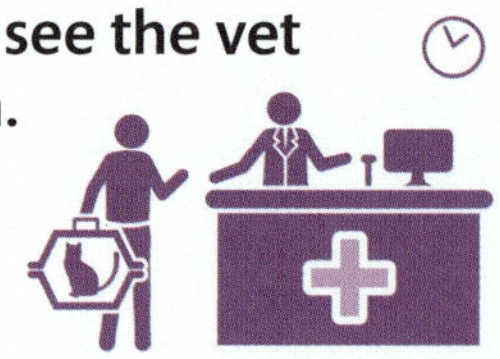

Kylie had a party to celebrate her 18th birthday. It was great fun!

Sean and Lisa had a talk about the new design for the office.

45.2 EXPRESSIONS WITH "GET"

You really need to **get going** if you want to catch the train.

Kyle and Erin **got lost** in the forest when they couldn't read their map.

I need to go to bed now. I'm **getting tired**.

I usually **get dressed** after I've eaten my breakfast.

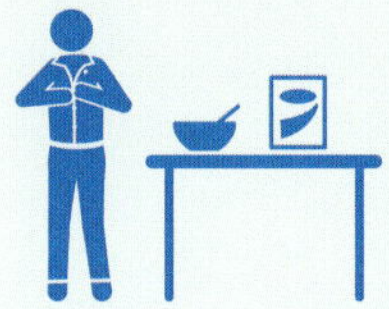

We finally **got home** at midnight after our flight was delayed.

Brian and Isha **got married** on a beautiful beach in Jamaica.

It was sunny today, but the weather is going to **get worse** tomorrow.

Claude is **getting better** at making cakes.

We finally **got started** on decorating the bedroom this morning.

Robin always **gets angry** when his children refuse to eat their food.

Aa 45.3 MARK THE SENTENCES THAT ARE CORRECT

Colin has a cold. He's staying at home today. ☑
Colin gets a cold. He's staying at home today. ☐

1 

After gardening all morning, we were so tired that we needed to have a rest. ☐
After gardening all morning, we were so tired that we needed to get a rest. ☐

2 

I need to go to bed now. I'm getting tired. ☐
I need to go to bed now. I'm having tired. ☐

3 

Shreya's going to get a baby this summer. ☐
Shreya's going to have a baby this summer. ☐

4 

Michael and Heather got an argument about the rules of the game. ☐
Michael and Heather had an argument about the rules of the game. ☐

5 

Lily had a conversation with another passenger on the train. ☐
Lily got a conversation with another passenger on the train. ☐

45.4 LISTEN TO THE AUDIO, THEN NUMBER THE PICTURES IN THE ORDER YOU HEAR THEM

A ☐

B ☐

C 1

D ☐

E ☐

F ☐

G ☐

H ☐

Aa 45.5 REWRITE THE SENTENCES, CORRECTING THE ERRORS

Shreya's going to **get a baby** this summer.

Shreya's going to have a baby this summer.

1 Robin always **has angry** when his children refuse to eat their food.

____

2 I **get an appointment** to see the vet at 2 o'clock this afternoon.

____

3 Sean and Lisa **got a talk** about the new design for the office.

____

4 Tiffany **got fun** at the festival with her friends.

____

Aa 45.6 LOOK AT THE PICTURES AND COMPLETE THE SENTENCES

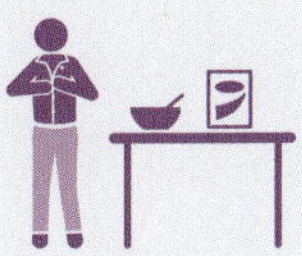

I usually *get dressed* after I've eaten my breakfast.

1 Kylie ______________ to celebrate her 18th birthday. It was great fun!

2 Claude is ______________ at making cakes.

3 I need to go to bed now. I'm ______________.

4 After gardening all morning, we were so tired that we needed to ______________.

5 You really need to ______________ if you want to catch the train.

46 "Set" and "put"

46.1 EXPRESSIONS WITH "SET"

I had a long way to drive, so I **set off** nice and early.

Catalina has **set the date** for her wedding next summer.

Ed **set the table** before his guests arrived for dinner.

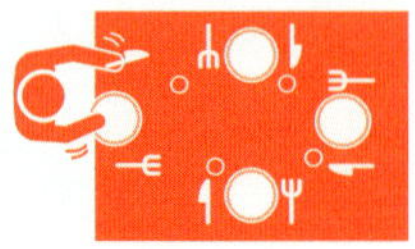

I **set a trap** to catch the mouse in the kitchen.

Mateo **set an example** for his children and ate all his vegetables.

I **set homework** for my students at the end of every lesson.

Silvio called the fire department after he accidentally **set fire** to his shed.

Judy was sad to see the birds trapped in their cage, so she **set them free**.

The ship **set sail** for China this morning. It will arrive in 20 days.

I have to get up early for work, so I always **set an alarm** before going to bed.

46.2 EXPRESSIONS WITH "PUT"

I always put off doing my homework until the last minute.

delay

My boss is putting pressure on me to sell all this kitchen equipment today.

trying to persuade someone to do something

Terry puts his family first. He always leaves work in time to meet his children after school.

gives one thing priority over everything else

The rangers have put a stop to people driving through the park to cut pollution.

made something stop happening

Irfan has put me in charge of the store while he is on vacation.

given me responsibility for

After telling my boss I was leaving my job, I put it in writing.

wrote it in a letter

Karen decided to put her cards on the table and tell Ricky that she loved him.

express her feelings openly

Sakura has been putting the heat on the contractors to finish the job quickly.

trying to force someone to do something

Seth isn't always the most hardworking employee. To put it bluntly, he's lazy.

say something simply and without being too polite

I really put my foot in it when I asked if Hazel was Tamsin's mother. They are actually sisters. (UK)

accidentally said something that upset someone

46.3 LISTEN TO THE AUDIO AND NUMBER THE SENTENCES IN THE ORDER YOU HEAR THEM

A My boss is putting pressure on me to sell all this kitchen equipment today. ☐

B Ed set the table before his guests arrived for dinner. [1]

C I have to get up early for work, so I always set an alarm before going to bed. ☐

D Irfan has put me in charge of the store while he is on vacation. ☐

E Mateo set an example for his children and ate all his vegetables. ☐

46.4 MATCH THE PICTURES TO THE CORRECT SENTENCES

After telling my boss I was leaving my job, I put it in writing.

1 

I always put off doing my homework until the last minute.

2 

Catalina has set the date for her wedding next summer.

3 

I had a long way to drive, so I set off nice and early.

4 

I set homework for my students at the end of every lesson.

46.5 MATCH THE EXPRESSIONS TO THEIR DEFINITIONS USING THE WORDS IN THE PANEL

put

put it in writing — wrote it in a letter

1 ______ express her feelings openly

2 ______ delay

3 ______ make something stop happening

4 ______ given me responsibility for

5 ______ say something simply

put off ~~put it in writing~~

put me in charge of put a stop to

put it bluntly put her cards on the table

Aa 46.6 CROSS OUT THE INCORRECT WORD IN EACH SENTENCE

I **set** / ~~**put**~~ a trap to catch the mouse in the kitchen.

1  I really **set** / **put** my foot in it when I asked if Hazel was Tamsin's mother. They are actually sisters.

2  Judy was sad to see the birds trapped in their cage, so she **set** / **put** them free.

3  The ship **set** / **put** sail for China this morning. It will arrive in 20 days.

4  Terry **sets** / **puts** his family first. He always leaves work in time to meet his children after school.

5  Sakura has been **setting** / **putting** the heat on the contractors to finish the job quickly.

Aa 46.7 MATCH THE BEGINNINGS OF THE SENTENCES TO THE CORRECT ENDINGS

	My boss is putting pressure on me	so I set off nice and early.
1	Silvio called the fire department	I put it in writing.
2	After telling my boss I was leaving my job,	to sell all this kitchen equipment today.
3	I had a long way to drive,	after he accidentally set fire to his shed.
4	I always put off doing my homework	the store while he is on vacation.
5	Ed set the table	until the last minute.
6	Irfan has put me in charge of	before his guests arrived for dinner.

47 "Go" and "come"

47.1 EXPRESSIONS WITH "GO"

Pavel likes to **go fishing** on Saturdays.

Dougie prefers to **go abroad** on vacation.

My kids **go crazy** whenever they hear that song.

My aunt's **going deaf**. You'll have to speak more loudly.

That style of shirt **went out of fashion** years ago!

This fruit has **gone bad**. It's not good to eat. (US)

My move **went smoothly**. I had lots of people helping me.

Everyone **went quiet** when the boss walked into the room.

Sara's fashion boutique **went bankrupt**. She couldn't afford the rent.

Joshua's dog has **gone missing**. He's putting up signs around town.

47.2 EXPRESSIONS WITH "COME"

The traffic came to a standstill because of a fallen tree on the road.

The climbers came close to reaching the peak but were too tired to continue.

The judges have come to a decision about the winner.

When the play came to an end, everyone left the theater.

Paula trained very hard and came in first in the hurdles. (US)

Riya came prepared for the camping trip.

The team has come to an agreement about which logo design to use.

Everyone thought Gabrielle would win the race, but she came in last. (US)

We were stranded on the rocks until the lifeguards came to the rescue.

As we walked through the mountains, a ruined castle came into view.

Aa 47.3 WRITE THE WORDS FROM THE PANEL UNDER THE CORRECT VERBS

GO	COME
bankrupt	

to a standstill	close	~~bankrupt~~	quiet
abroad	to a decision	into view	fishing
deaf	to an agreement	crazy	in last
prepared	to the rescue	missing	bad

Aa 47.4 MATCH THE PICTURES TO THE CORRECT SENTENCES

1 

2 

3 

4 

My kids go crazy whenever they hear that song.

This fruit has gone bad. It's not good to eat.

That style of shirt went out of fashion years ago!

Riya came prepared for the camping trip.

When the play came to an end, everyone left the theater.

47.5 LISTEN TO THE AUDIO, THEN NUMBER THE SENTENCES IN THE ORDER YOU HEAR THEM

A The climbers came close to reaching the peak but were too tired to continue. ☐

B Everyone thought Gabrielle would win the race, but she came in last. *1*

C Pavel likes to go fishing on Saturdays. ☐

D My move went smoothly. I had lots of people helping me. ☐

E As we walked through the mountains, a ruined castle came into view. ☐

F The traffic came to a standstill because of a fallen tree on the road. ☐

Aa 47.6 CROSS OUT THE INCORRECT WORD IN EACH SENTENCE

We were stranded on the rocks until the lifeguards ~~went~~ / came to the rescue.

1. This fruit has gone / come bad. It's not good to eat.
2. My aunt's going / coming deaf. You'll have to speak more loudly.
3. The judges have gone / come to a decision about the winner.
4. Sara's fashion boutique went / came bankrupt. She couldn't afford the rent.
5. Everyone went / came quiet when the boss walked into the room.
6. My move went / came smoothly. I had lots of people helping me.
7. The team has gone / come to an agreement about which logo design to use.

Aa 47.7 LOOK AT THE PICTURES AND COMPLETE THE SENTENCES

As we walked through the mountains, a ruined castle *came into view*.

1. Joshua's dog has ________________.
He's putting up signs around town.

2. We were stranded on the rocks until the lifeguards ________________.

3. Dougie prefers to ________________ on vacation.

4. Pavel likes to ________________ on Saturdays.

5. Paula trained very hard and ________________ ________________ in the hurdles.

48 Expressions with other verbs

48.1 EXPRESSIONS WITH "PAY"

I live with my parents, but pay my way by buying groceries.

contribute toward the cost of something

The children paid close attention to John as he told them about his travels.

listened or watched carefully

When our CEO retired, Nisha paid tribute to her with a wonderful speech.

publicly praised someone for their achievements

Kelly paid me a compliment and said she liked my new haircut.

said something nice about me

Two firefighters paid a visit to my son's school today to talk about fire safety.

visited

It was so kind of you to lend me that money to get my car fixed. I can pay you back now.

repay a loan

48.2 EXPRESSIONS WITH "HOLD"

We hold a meeting each Monday to discuss the week ahead.

have a meeting

Mark holds a grudge against me because I didn't give him a promotion last year.

is still angry about something that happened a long time ago

I had to hold my tongue when Julian showed me his new suit. It was horrible!

avoid saying what I really thought

I'm trying to call the bank and they've asked me to hold the line. It's so annoying! (UK)

wait for a telephone conversation to continue

48.3 EXPRESSIONS WITH "CATCH"

Raul caught a glimpse of a deer as he hiked through the forest.

saw very briefly

I must have caught a cold from that man who couldn't stop sneezing on the train.

become sick with a cold

After climbing the stairs, I stopped to catch my breath.

rest after exercise and breathe more slowly

We need to tell the waiter we're ready to order. Let's try and catch his eye.

get his attention

Don't stand so close to the stove. Your clothes could catch fire!

start to burn

Pari usually drives to work, but she caught the train this morning.

traveled by train

48.4 EXPRESSIONS WITH "KEEP"

It's important to keep your distance when you drive on busy roads.

Cleo told me about her mom's surprise party but asked me to keep it a secret.

Natalie always keeps calm when she has to talk to angry customers.

The teacher asked the students to keep quiet during the test.

Aa 48.5 CROSS OUT THE INCORRECT WORDS IN EACH SENTENCE

Mark ~~pays~~ / **holds** / ~~keeps~~ a grudge against me because I didn't give him a promotion last year.

1. Two firefighters **paid** / **held** / **kept** a visit to my son's school today to talk about fire safety.
2. I'm trying to call the bank and they've asked me to **hold** / **catch** / **keep** the line. It's so annoying!
3. Cleo told me about her mom's surprise party but asked me to **hold** / **catch** / **keep** it a secret.
4. We **pay** / **hold** / **keep** a meeting each Monday to discuss the week ahead.

Aa 48.6 MATCH THE EXPRESSIONS TO THEIR DEFINITIONS USING THE WORDS IN THE PANEL

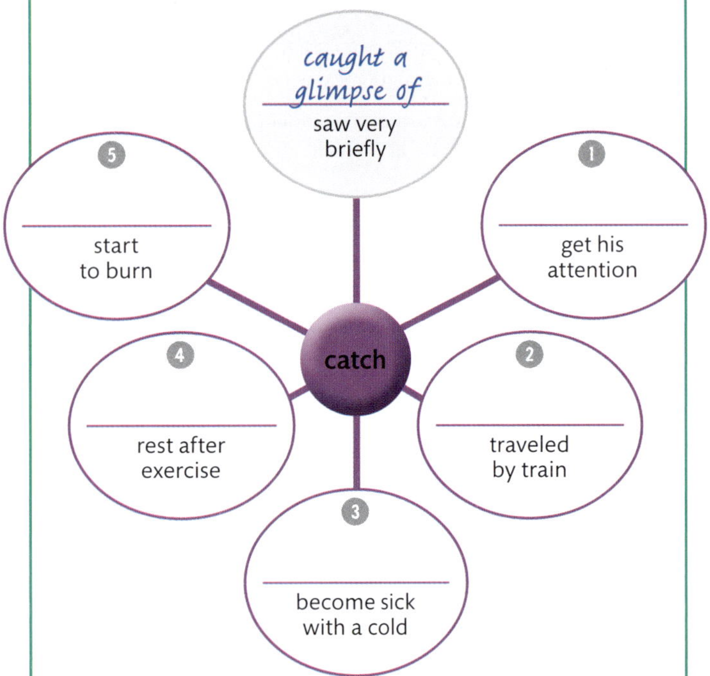

caught a cold | caught the train
catch fire | ~~caught a glimpse of~~
catch his eye | catch my breath

48.7 LISTEN TO THE AUDIO AND MARK THE CORRECT PICTURE FOR EACH SENTENCE YOU HEAR

1. 
2. 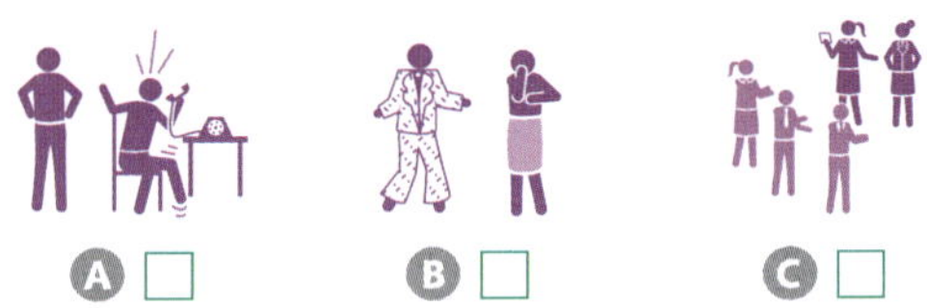
3. 
4. 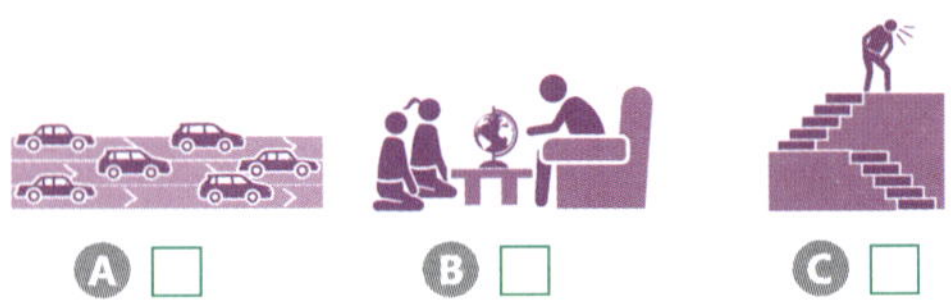

Aa 48.8 MATCH THE BEGINNINGS OF THE SENTENCES TO THE CORRECT ENDINGS

It's important to keep your → distance when you drive on busy roads.

1. The teacher asked the students
2. The children paid close attention to John
3. I live with my parents, but
4. Natalie always keeps calm
5. After climbing the stairs,
6. Pari usually drives to work,
7. Raul caught a glimpse of
8. Kelly paid me a compliment

- to keep quiet during the test.
- pay my way by buying groceries.
- distance when you drive on busy roads.
- and said she liked my new haircut.
- as he told them about his travels.
- but she caught the train this morning.
- a deer as he hiked through the forest.
- I stopped to catch my breath.
- when she has to talk to angry customers.

Aa 48.9 WRITE THE CORRECT EXPRESSION NEXT TO ITS DEFINITION

contribute toward the cost of something = *pay my way*

1. repay a loan = ______
2. publicly praised someone for their achievements = ______
3. avoid saying what I really thought = ______
4. wait for a telephone conversation to continue = ______
5. said something nice about me = ______
6. is still angry about something that happened a long time ago = ______
7. listened or watched carefully = ______

49 Intensifying adverbs

49.1 "ABSOLUTELY"

Use "absolutely" to intensify a statement that expresses an opinion.

This food is **absolutely delicious**. You're such a good cook!

The park is **absolutely beautiful** at this time of year.

Xavier's old computer was **absolutely useless**. He decided to throw it away.

The weather was **absolutely fantastic** when we went to Barbados. It was sunny every day.

49.2 "HIGHLY"

Use "highly" to intensify a statement about probability or praise.

It is **highly probable** that Leo is going to lose his job.

I **highly recommend** this book. I stayed up all night reading it!

It is **highly unlikely** that I'll be well enough to go to work tomorrow.

Cesar's new movie was **highly praised** by the critics.

49.3 "DEEPLY"

Use "deeply" to intensify a statement about emotions.

I was **deeply hurt** when Madison didn't invite me to her wedding.

Gina was **deeply concerned** when her cat didn't come home for his dinner.

49.4 "STRONGLY"

Use "strongly" to intensify advice or a statement about beliefs and values.

We **strongly advise** you not to travel unless it is absolutely necessary.

Malachi **strongly believes** in looking after the environment.

My uncle **strongly feels** that children shouldn't watch too much television.

49.5 "UNBELIEVABLY"

Use "unbelievably" to intensify a statement about extreme or unlikely situations.

I was **unbelievably lucky** to get my violin back after I left it on the train.

Some people can be **unbelievably selfish** when they are on the bus.

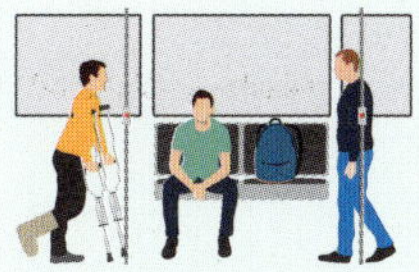

That date was **unbelievably awkward**. We had nothing to say to each other.

49.6 "RIDICULOUSLY"

Use "ridiculously" to intensify criticism or a statement of disbelief.

The clothes in that store are **ridiculously expensive**.

Sadie finished the test early. She thought it was **ridiculously easy**.

The portions in this restaurant are **ridiculously small**.

André gets up **ridiculously early** every morning.

49.7 LISTEN TO THE AUDIO AND COMPLETE THE SENTENCES THAT DESCRIBE EACH PICTURE

I *highly recommend* this book. I stayed up all night reading it!

1 André gets up ______________________ every morning.

2 This food is ______________________. You're such a good cook!

3 We ______________ you not to travel unless it is absolutely necessary.

4 That date was ______________________. We had nothing to say to each other.

5 Gina was ______________ when her cat didn't come home for his dinner.

Aa 49.8 MATCH THE BEGINNINGS OF THE SENTENCES TO THE CORRECT ENDINGS

	The clothes in that store	at this time of year.
1	Cesar's new movie was	didn't invite me to her wedding.
2	The park is absolutely beautiful	are ridiculously expensive.
3	I was deeply hurt when Madison	highly praised by the critics.
4	The portions in this restaurant	looking after the environment.
5	Malachi strongly believes in	are ridiculously small.

Aa 49.9 WRITE THE WORDS FROM THE PANEL UNDER THE CORRECT ADVERB

ABSOLUTELY	HIGHLY	RIDICULOUSLY	STRONGLY
delicious			

unlikely easy ~~delicious~~ expensive believes probable
useless praised early feels fantastic advise

Aa 49.10 CROSS OUT THE INCORRECT WORDS IN EACH SENTENCE

I was ~~highly~~ / **deeply** / ~~strongly~~ hurt when Madison didn't invite me to her wedding.

1 

I was **absolutely** / **strongly** / **unbelievably** lucky to get my violin back after I left it on the train.

2 

Gina was **deeply** / **highly** / **absolutely** concerned when her cat didn't come home for his dinner.

3 

I **highly** / **ridiculously** / **deeply** recommend this book. I stayed up all night reading it!

4 

Some people can be **absolutely** / **unbelievably** / **strongly** selfish when they are on the bus.

5 

Malachi **strongly** / **highly** / **deeply** believes in looking after the environment.

50 Similes

50.1 SIMILES WITH "AS"

Mary's car is **as old as the hills**. She refuses to buy a new one.

My grandmother is **as deaf as a post**. She always turns up the TV really loud.

Andrei went **as white as a sheet** when he saw a spider in his bedroom.

The children were **as good as gold** while they stayed with their grandmother.

Have you been out in the snow? Your hands are **as cold as ice**!

These new high-speed trains are great! They're **as fast as lightning**.

I don't need help carrying my bag. It's **as light as a feather**.

There was no rain for months, and the land was **as dry as a bone**.

50.3 SIMILES WITH "LIKE"

Selma **slept like a log** after a long day climbing in the Alps.

Roy's new suit **fits like a glove**. He looks really good.

50.2 SIMILES USING VOCABULARY ABOUT ANIMALS

Paul is as quiet as a mouse.
He never talks in meetings.

Naomi was as brave as a lion and confronted the school bully in the playground.

I'm recovering from the flu, and I still feel as weak as a kitten.

My grandfather is as wise as an owl.
He always gives good advice.

Javier was as busy as a bee getting ready for the party.

I'm as blind as a bat without my glasses.

Fiona looked as proud as a peacock in her new hat.

My uncle is as strong as an ox.
He's a champion weightlifter.

I was shaking like a leaf before I went into the cave.

We had to run like the wind to catch that bus!

Aa 50.4 CROSS OUT THE INCORRECT WORDS IN EACH SENTENCE

We had to run like the ~~fire~~ / ~~water~~ / **wind** to catch that bus!

1  I don't need help carrying my bag. It's as light as a **bird** / **mouse** / **feather**.

2  My uncle is as strong as an **eagle** / **ox** / **elephant**. He's a champion weightlifter.

3  My grandfather is as **wise** / **clever** / **bright** as an owl. He always gives good advice.

4  I'm as blind as a **mole** / **bat** / **worm** without my glasses.

5  Paul is as quiet as a **mouse** / **sheep** / **fish**. He never talks in meetings.

Aa 50.5 FILL IN THE GAPS, PUTTING THE WORDS IN THE CORRECT ORDER

a | weak | as | kitten | as

I'm recovering from the flu, and I still feel *as* *weak* *as* *a* *kitten* .

bone | as | dry | a | as

1 There was no rain for months, and the land was ______ ______ ______ ______ ______ .

a | as | peacock | as | proud

2 Fiona looked ______ ______ ______ ______ ______ in her new hat.

hills | old | as | the | as

3 Mary's car is ______ ______ ______ ______ ______ . She refuses to buy a new one.

like | log | a | slept

4 Selma ______ ______ ______ ______ after a long day climbing in the Alps.

Aa 50.6 MATCH THE BEGINNINGS OF THE SIMILES TO THE CORRECT ENDINGS

	as strong → as an ox	as gold
1	as good	as a post
2	as deaf	as an ox
3	shaking	as lightning
4	as white	like a leaf
5	as fast	as a lion
6	as brave	as a sheet

50.7 LISTEN TO THE AUDIO AND MARK THE SIMILES YOU HEAR

- A as proud as a peacock ☑
- B as light as a feather ☐
- C as weak as a kitten ☐
- D as cold as ice ☐
- E as wise as an owl ☐
- F as blind as a bat ☐
- G as white as a sheet ☐
- H run like the wind ☐
- I as quiet as a mouse ☐

Aa 50.8 LOOK AT THE PICTURES AND COMPLETE THE SENTENCES USING SIMILES

Selma *slept like a log* after a long day climbing in the Alps.

1 Have you been out in the snow? Your hands are ______________________ !

2 Mary's car is ______________________ ______ . She refuses to buy a new one.

3 Javier was ______________________ getting ready for the party.

4 Roy's new suit ______________________ . He looks really good.

5 My grandmother is ______________________ ______ . She always turns up the TV really loud.

51 Proverbs

51.1 COMMON ENGLISH PROVERBS

Don't go into that spooky house! Curiosity killed the cat.

Being too curious can get you into trouble.

Azra adores her pet snake. I suppose beauty is in the eye of the beholder.

everyone has their own idea of what is beautiful

I can't follow directions unless I have a map. A picture is worth a thousand words.

It is easier to show something in a picture than to describe it using words.

Jakob really misses his girlfriend now that she has gone to college. Absence makes the heart grow fonder.

Being away from someone you love makes you love them more.

Don't just say you're going to clean your room, do it! Actions speak louder than words.

What you do matters more than what you say.

I was so pleased when I finally managed to sell my house for a good price. All good things come to those who wait.

If you wait for something good, you will eventually get it.

You were meant to give me this assignment a week ago, but better late than never.

it's better for something to happen late than not to happen at all

Flo's incompetence at work is affecting the whole team. A chain is only as strong as its weakest link.

A team is only as strong as its weakest member.

Don't count your chickens before they hatch, Kim! The game isn't over yet.

don't assume that something will happen before the outcome is certain

Stop sitting by the phone waiting to hear if you got the job. A watched pot never boils.

Time will pass more quickly if you keep busy while you're waiting for something.

Stop complaining about your toothache and call the dentist. There's no time like the present.

It's better to do things now than wait.

I asked Sofia to help me write this difficult report. Two heads are better than one.

It's helpful to have the advice of a second person.

I'm so glad I told Amira I was stressed at work. A problem shared is a problem halved.

If you tell someone about a problem, you'll feel better.

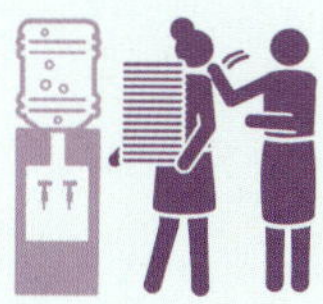

The day the sales began, Tamsin was outside the store at 6 in the morning. The early bird catches the worm.

The person who arrives early or acts quickly will get what they want.

Logan said the shelf fell down because his drill was broken, but a bad workman always blames his tools.

people who are bad at something blame the equipment they use

I've been playing the trumpet every day and I'm really improving. Practice makes perfect.

Practicing something will make you very good at it.

I told Sam about a great job, but he didn't apply. You can lead a horse to water, but you can't make it drink.

You can make something easier for someone, but you can't force them to do it.

We're almost ready for the party and we've still got plenty of time. Many hands make light work.

Things get done quickly when lots of people help.

I know he looks a bit scary, but my dog's really gentle. You can't judge a book by its cover.

You shouldn't make judgments based on appearance.

I think you should tell Carlo that it was you who broke his skateboard. Honesty is the best policy.

It's always better to tell the truth.

Aa 51.2 MATCH THE BEGINNINGS OF THE PROVERBS TO THE CORRECT ENDINGS

The early bird → catches the worm.

1. Honesty is
2. Many hands
3. There's no time
4. Two heads are
5. Curiosity killed
6. Better late
7. Actions speak

- better than one.
- make light work.
- catches the worm.
- the best policy.
- than never.
- like the present.
- louder than words.
- the cat.

51.3 LISTEN TO THE AUDIO, THEN NUMBER THE PICTURES IN THE ORDER YOU HEAR THEM

A ☐

B ☐

C ☐

D ☐

E ☐

F 1

G ☐

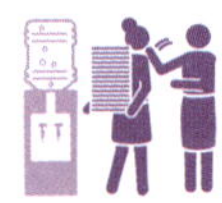
H ☐

I ☐

Aa 51.4 REWRITE THE SENTENCES, CORRECTING THE ERRORS

Don't just say you're going to clean your room, do it! **Actions talk louder than words.**

Don't just say you're going to clean your room, do it! Actions speak louder than words.

1. **Don't count your geese before they hatch**, Kim! The game isn't over yet.

____

2. Stop sitting by the phone waiting to hear if you got the job. **A watched kettle never boils.**

____

3. I've been playing the trumpet every day and I'm really improving. **Practice becomes perfect.**

____

4. Azra adores her pet snake. I suppose **beauty is in the eye of the owner.**

____

Aa 51.5 MATCH THE PICTURES TO THE CORRECT SENTENCES

1 

2 

3 

4 

5 

Flo's incompetence at work is affecting the whole team. A chain is only as strong as its weakest link.

I asked Sofia to help me write this difficult report. Two heads are better than one.

Jakob really misses his girlfriend now that she has gone to college. Absence makes the heart grow fonder.

We're almost ready for the party and we've still got plenty of time. Many hands make light work.

You were meant to give me this assignment a week ago, but better late than never.

The day the sales began, Tamsin was outside the store at 6 in the morning. The early bird catches the worm!

Aa 51.6 WRITE THE CORRECT PROVERB NEXT TO ITS DEFINITION

Things get done quickly when lots of people help. = *Many hands make light work.*

1. It's better to do things now than wait. = ______________________
2. It's always better to tell the truth. = ______________________
3. Being too curious can get you into trouble. = ______________________
4. What you do matters more than what you say. = ______________________

52 Easily confused words 1

52.1 "LOOK AT," "SEE," AND "WATCH"

Use "look at" to talk about paying attention to something or someone.

Come outside and look at the flowers I planted last month.

Use "see" to talk about noticing something.

I saw Keiko's large ginger cat lying on the lawn.

Use "watch" to talk about observing something over a period of time.

The cat watched the birds sitting in a tree.

52.2 "WAIT," "EXPECT," AND "LOOK FORWARD TO"

Use "wait" to talk about staying in the same place before something happens.

I'm going to a party tonight. I've been waiting for the bus for 10 minutes.

Use "expect" to talk about what people think will happen in the future.

I expect that there will be lots of people at the party.

Use "look forward to" to talk about feeling excited about a future event.

I'm really looking forward to seeing the fireworks display at the party.

52.3 "LISTEN TO" AND "HEAR"

Use "listen to" to talk about paying attention over a period of time to a sound.

Jules often listens to music on his walk home from work.

Use "hear" to talk about suddenly noticing a sound.

Suddenly, Jules heard a loud bang coming from behind him.

52.4 "WIN" AND "BEAT"

Use "win" to talk about achieving or gaining something.

The Lions have won the soccer championship again.

Use "beat" to talk about a victory over an opponent.

The Lions beat the Stars 3–1.

52.5 "BORROW" AND "LEND"

Use "borrow" to talk about receiving something for a short time.

My laptop's broken and I have to apply for a job tonight. Could I borrow yours, please?

Use "lend" to talk about giving something to someone else for a short time.

Yes, I will lend you my laptop, but please be careful with it.

52.6 "WISH" AND "HOPE"

Use "wish" to talk about situations that you would like to happen but are impossible.

I wish my test results were better.

Use "hope" to talk about situations that are still possible in the future.

I hope I still get into college.

52.7 "SMELL" AND "FEEL"

Use "smell" to talk about the scent or odor of something.

This pie that you've been baking smells delicious!

Use "feel" to talk about experiencing a sensation or emotion.

It's making me feel hungry.

Aa 52.8 CROSS OUT THE INCORRECT WORD IN EACH SENTENCE

The Lions have **won** / ~~**beaten**~~ the soccer championship again.

1  Yes, I will **borrow** / **lend** you my laptop, but please be careful with it.

2  I **wait** / **expect** that there will be lots of people at the party.

3  I **wish** / **hope** I still get into college.

4  Suddenly, Jules **listened to** / **heard** a loud bang coming from behind him.

5  This pie that you've been baking **smells** / **feels** delicious!

Aa 52.9 FILL IN THE GAPS USING THE WORDS IN THE PANEL

I'm really *looking forward to* seeing the fireworks display at the party.

1 Jules often ____________________ music on his walk home from work.

2 Come outside and ____________________ the flowers I planted last month.

3 The Lions have ____________________ the soccer championship again.

4 The Lions ____________________ the Stars 3–1.

5 I ____________________ Keiko's large ginger cat lying on the lawn.

won | listens to | saw | look at | ~~looking forward to~~ | beat

52.10 MATCH THE BEGINNINGS OF THE SENTENCES TO THE CORRECT ENDINGS

Yes, I will lend you my laptop, → but please be careful with it.

1. The cat watched the birds
2. I wish my
3. This pie that you've been baking
4. Suddenly, Jules heard a loud bang
5. I expect that there will be
6. Come outside and look at
7. The Lions have won
8. I'm really looking forward to
9. Jules often listens to

- test results were better.
- lots of people at the party.
- but please be careful with it.
- the flowers I planted last month.
- sitting in a tree.
- coming from behind him.
- smells delicious!
- seeing the fireworks display at the party.
- music on his walk home from work.
- the soccer championship again.

52.11 LISTEN TO THE AUDIO, THEN NUMBER THE PICTURES IN THE ORDER YOU HEAR THEM

A ☐

B ☐

C [1]

D ☐

E ☐

F ☐

G ☐

H ☐

53 Easily confused words 2

53.1 "DAMAGE," "INJURE," AND "HURT"

Use "damage" to talk about causing harm to an object or thing.

Colm damaged Sheila's vase when he dropped it.

Use "injure" (or "hurt") to talk about causing harm or pain to a person or a part of the body.

Colm injured his foot when he dropped the vase.

Use "hurt" to talk about feeling pain. You can't use "injure" to talk about feeling pain.

Colm's foot still hurt for days after the accident.

53.2 "LOAD," "FILL UP," AND "CHARGE"

Use "load" to talk about putting objects into something, usually a vehicle.

Can you help me load the car with everything we need for the beach?

Use "fill up" or "fill" to talk about putting something, usually a liquid, into a container.

Don't forget to bring water. I'll fill up some bottles for us.

Use "charge" to talk about giving a battery-operated device electricity that can be stored.

Wait a minute! I need to charge my phone before we go.

53.3 "SAY" AND "TELL"

When you use "say," you don't have to state who a person is talking to.

"Oh, no," said Kayleigh. "I've left my school bag on the bus with all my homework in it."

When you use "tell," you must state who a person is talking to.

Kayleigh had to tell her teacher that she had left her homework on the bus.

53.4 "WEAR" AND "CARRY"

Use "wear" to talk about having clothing on your body.

Nina wore her new dress to Jack's party.

Use "carry" to talk about bringing an object from one place to another.

Arnold carried Jack's birthday cake into the dining room.

53.5 "REMIND" AND "REMEMBER"

Use "remind" to talk about making someone remember something.

Silvia reminded Sanjay to visit his mother on her birthday.

Use "remember" to talk about keeping something in your mind.

Sanjay remembered to visit his mother, who was delighted to see him.

53.6 "SENSIBLE" AND "SENSITIVE"

Use "sensible" to describe a person or a course of action that shows good judgment.

Are you sure you want to buy that car? It would be more sensible to save your money.

Use "sensitive" to describe a person who feels emotions strongly and easily gets upset.

There's no need to be so sensitive! I was only trying to give you advice.

53.7 "JOB" AND "WORK"

Use "job" to describe the specific role someone has in a workplace.

I have a job as a sales assistant in a supermarket.

Use "work" to talk about the activities that someone carries out in a workplace.

There is lots of work to do. I have to stack shelves and serve customers.

Aa 53.8 MATCH THE PICTURES TO THE CORRECT SENTENCES

"Oh, no," said Kayleigh. "I've left my school bag on the bus with all my homework in it."

Sanjay remembered to visit his mother, who was delighted to see him.

1 

There is lots of work to do. I have to stack shelves and serve customers.

2 

Are you sure you want to buy that car? It would be more sensible to save your money.

3 

Colm injured his foot when he dropped the vase.

4 

Aa 53.9 MARK THE SENTENCES THAT ARE CORRECT

Kayleigh had to say her teacher that she had left her homework on the bus. ☐
Kayleigh had to tell her teacher that she had left her homework on the bus. ☑

1. Colm's foot still hurt for days after the accident. ☐
   Colm's foot still injured for days after the accident. ☐

2. Wait a minute! I need to load my phone before we go. ☐
   Wait a minute! I need to charge my phone before we go. ☐

3. Silvia remembered Sanjay to visit his mother on her birthday. ☐
   Silvia reminded Sanjay to visit his mother on her birthday. ☐

4. I have a job as a sales assistant in a supermarket. ☐
   I have a work as a sales assistant in a supermarket. ☐

53.10 LISTEN TO THE AUDIO, THEN NUMBER THE SENTENCES IN THE ORDER YOU HEAR THEM

A. Don't forget to bring water. I'll fill up some bottles for us. ☐

B. Arnold carried Jack's birthday cake into the dining room. ☐

C. Colm injured his foot when he dropped the vase. ☐

D. Can you help me load the car with everything we need for the beach? ☐

E. Colm's foot still hurt for days after the accident. ☐

F. Colm damaged Sheila's vase when he dropped it. ☐

G. Nina wore her new dress to Jack's party. [1]

H. Wait a minute! I need to charge my phone before we go. ☐

53.11 REWRITE THE SENTENCES, CORRECTING THE ERRORS

I have a **work** as a sales assistant in a supermarket.
I have a job as a sales assistant in a supermarket.

1. There's no need to be so **sensible**! I was only trying to give you advice.

2. Kayleigh had to **say** her teacher that she had left her homework on the bus.

3. Colm **injured** Sheila's vase when he dropped it.

4. Sanjay **reminded** to visit his mother, who was delighted to see him.

5. Nina **carried** her new dress to Jack's party.

6. Don't forget to bring water. I'll **load** some bottles for us.

54 Colors

54.1 IDIOMS USING VOCABULARY ABOUT COLORS

The party was a black-tie event and everyone was really well dressed.

an event for which people have to dress very formally

Paula has a green thumb. She has so many beautiful plants in her house. (US)

a talent for gardening

The day I received my degree was a red-letter day for me.

an important or happy day

The actress made her first appearance on the silver screen in the 1950s.

in a movie

Sergio got a black eye after he walked into a lamppost.

a bruise around the eye

Layla was green with envy when her brother won the lottery.

very jealous

Alyssa knocked on my door out of the blue yesterday. I hadn't seen her for years!

unexpectedly

We're protesting against plans to build houses on the green belt in our local area.

fields or parks around a town or city

I hate the winter! It's only 4 o'clock and it's already pitch black outside.

very dark

It's my birthday, so I'm going to paint the town red with my friends tonight.

go out and celebrate enthusiastically

Fake designer goods are sold on the black market.

the illegal buying and selling of goods

I thought my new boss was really nice, but he showed his true colors when I forgot to put sugar in his coffee.

showed his real character and feelings

Ela turned beet-red when I caught her copying my homework. (US)

blushed, was very embarrassed

Larry was black and blue after falling down the stairs.

badly bruised

Jo saw red when she found her sister wearing her sweater.

became angry

Francis only cleans his house once in a blue moon.

very rarely

There's a gray area in the office dress code. My boss said it was casual, but she told me I couldn't wear shorts.

a situation where the rules are unclear

I want to be a teacher, so getting work experience at the school was a golden opportunity for me.

a good chance to do something rewarding or get something valuable

The boys were caught red-handed when they tried to break into the house.

caught doing something wrong

I always get the blues when my vacation is over and I have to go back to work.

feel sad

54.2 LISTEN TO THE AUDIO AND MARK THE IDIOMS YOU HEAR

a black eye ☑	saw red ☐	a gray area ☐
1 a red-letter day ☐	paint the town red ☐	saw red ☐
2 black and blue ☐	out of the blue ☐	pitch black ☐
3 a gray area ☐	a green thumb ☐	the green belt ☐
4 black and blue ☐	a black eye ☐	out of the blue ☐
5 turned beet-red ☐	saw red ☐	caught red-handed ☐
6 a black-tie event ☐	black and blue ☐	pitch black ☐
7 green with envy ☐	a green thumb ☐	the green belt ☐

54.3 READ THE LETTER AND CROSS OUT THE INCORRECT WORDS

Hi Sandra,

Alyssa knocked on my door out of the blue / ~~green~~ yesterday. I hadn't seen her for years! She said she was going to paint the town gold / red for her birthday next week, and invited me along, too. You know I only go out once in a white / blue moon, so I thought it would be a silver / golden opportunity to meet some new friends. She said I could bring a friend along. Would you like to come with me?

Love,

Janice

54.4 REWRITE THE SENTENCES, CORRECTING THE ERRORS

Francis only cleans his house **once in a pink moon**.

Francis only cleans his house once in a blue moon.

1 Sergio got **a blue eye** after he walked into a lamppost.

2 The actress made her first appearance **on the golden screen** in the 1950s.

3 I always **get the grays** when my vacation is over and I have to go back to work.

4 The boys were **caught blue-handed** when they tried to break into the house.

54.5 MATCH THE PICTURES TO THE CORRECT SENTENCES

There's a gray area in the office dress code. My boss said it was casual, but she told me I couldn't wear shorts.

It's my birthday, so I'm going to paint the town red with my friends tonight.

1 

I thought my new boss was really nice, but he showed his true colors when I forgot to put sugar in his coffee.

2 

I want to be a teacher, so getting work experience at the school was a golden opportunity for me.

3 

We're protesting against plans to build houses on the green belt in our local area.

4 

Fake designer goods are sold on the black market.

5 

54.6 WRITE THE CORRECT IDIOM NEXT TO ITS DEFINITION, FILLING IN THE MISSING LETTERS

an important or happy day = a red-letter day

1. badly bruised = b _ _ _ _ a _ _ b _ _ _
2. became angry = s _ _ r _ _
3. a talent for gardening = a g _ _ _ _ t _ _ _ _
4. very jealous = g _ _ _ _ w _ _ _ e _ _ _
5. unexpectedly = o _ _ o _ t _ _ b _ _ _

Answers

01

1.3

YOUNG:
bright young things
tender age
knee-high to a grasshopper

OLD:
no spring chicken
over the hill
great age

1.4

1 Becky's worried she's **getting on in years** after spotting more gray hairs.
2 Damien's at **that awkward age** and finds it hard to talk to people.
3 My grandpa got married again at the **ripe old age** of 92.
4 This TV show **bridges the generation gap**. The whole family loves it.
5 I **feel my age** when I go shopping with my children.

1.5

1 I'm too **long in the tooth** to try out skydiving.
2 My assistant is a bit **wet behind the ears**. He still has a lot to learn.
3 Derek and Joan spent their **twilight years** traveling the world.
4 In many countries, there is a big celebration when young people **come of age**.
5 Angela might be 84, but she is still **young at heart**.
6 Sanjay feels **as old as the hills** when his kids talk about technology.

1.6

1 improve with age
2 over the hill
3 great age
4 twilight years
5 young at heart
6 tender age

02

2.3

1 a family heirloom
2 a fair-weather friend
3 losing touch with
4 a soulmate
5 drifted apart
6 extended family

2.4

A 6 B 4 C 1 D 7 E 2 F 8 G 5 H 3

2.5

1 We're moving to a bigger house because we're hoping to **start** a family soon.
2 My wife and I **hit** it off immediately when we first met at a country music concert.
3 Uncle Tony is the black **sheep** of the family. He's been to prison three times.
4 Cy and I got off on the wrong **foot** on our date. He was an hour late and forgot my name.
5 Ramón and Tara get on like a **house** on fire. They're always talking and laughing.

2.6

1 We're **bringing up** our children to be kind to animals.
2 Marie and Pierre met through Isaac, **a mutual friend** of theirs.
3 Curly hair **runs in our family**, and my daughter, mom, and I all have it.
4 I've **kept in touch with** Lin since we left college 25 years ago.
5 Jade is **a family friend**. She grew up on the same street as us.

03

3.4

1 My aunt is a well-respected person.
2 Philip has always been wealthy.
3 Bob is from the wrong social background.
4 Clara looked extremely glamorous.
5 She is descended from important people.

3.5

1 Edie **looks like butter wouldn't melt in her mouth**, but she's actually really naughty.
2 Oscar is only 25, but he's already **getting thin on top**.
3 My aunt believed in **keeping up appearances** despite having little money.
4 Nalini **never has a hair out of place**. She cares a lot about her appearance.
5 Milan returned home with **five o'clock shadow** after a long day at the office.

3.6

1 Domenica **looked the part** for her first day of work at the bank.
2 Clara **looked like a million bucks** when she arrived for her wedding.
3 Mateo and his brother Lucas are **like two peas in a pod**. I can't tell them apart.
4 Karen is **the spitting image of** that actor in the new sci-fi film.
5 Rita **looked like she'd seen a ghost** after I told her my news.
6 Rachel **looked like a drowned rat** after she got caught in the rain on her way home.

3.7

1 all skin and bones
2 the spitting image of
3 getting thin on top
4 five o'clock shadow
5 a highflier

04

4.4

1 It was great to see Jasmine at the party. She's always a barrel of laughs.
2 Bob is such a crybaby. He was very upset about not getting a perfect score.
3 Don't be afraid of Linda. Her bark is worse than her bite.
4 Jim's a good egg. He helped me to move last week.
5 Gustav has a selfish streak. He won't share his cookies with his friends.
6 Debbie's a tough cookie. She doesn't mind when people criticize her work.

4.5

A 4 B 6 C 2 D 1 E 8 F 3 G 5 H 7

4.6

1 Noah is really down to earth. He earns lots of money, but he lives in a little cottage.
2 My dad's just an average Joe. He enjoys burgers and fries, and he loves watching baseball.
3 Tony wouldn't say boo to a goose. He gets really shy when he talks to customers.
4 Norah is such a fuddy-duddy. She never wants to come out with us on Saturday night.
5 Arturo is so two-faced. He said he liked my haircut but told his friends he hated it.

4.7

1 Her bark is worse than her bite.
2 as cool as a cucumber
3 as bold as brass
4 a barrel of laughs
5 wouldn't hurt a fly

05

5.2

1 My kids think this TV show is **the best thing since sliced bread**.
2 We had a wonderful boat trip. **The icing on the cake** was seeing some dolphins.
3 Chan's store only sells watches that are **top of the line**.
4 **The crème de la crème** of the fashion world were at the launch party.

5.3

A 2 B 6 C 1 D 5 E 4 F 3

5.4
1 out of this world
2 the best of both worlds
3 second to none
4 stole the show
5 the crème de la crème
6 the bee's knees
7 a blessing in disguise

5.5
1 highest quality
2 the best part of a good experience
3 excellent reviews
4 really likes or admires
5 that she has fantasized about having

5.6
1 **World-class** athletes need to train for a few hours every day.
2 Marcelo **stole the show** with his amazing singing.
3 **The crème de la crème** of the fashion world were at the launch party.
4 Walking to work gives me **the best of both worlds**. It helps me save money and get fit.
5 The burgers in Max's diner are **to die for**. And they're huge!

06

6.2
1 cheap and nasty
2 like watching paint dry
3 past its sell-by date
4 a fate worse than death
5 not my cup of tea
6 rough around the edges

6.3
1 The museum in my town is nothing to **write** home about. There are very few exhibits.
2 The weather in Hawaii didn't **live** up to expectations. It rained every day.
3 Rita's TV is on its last **legs**. She's had it for over 10 years.
4 The clothes in this store are second **rate**. They don't last very long.
5 Pete's habit of dropping litter leaves a bad **taste** in my mouth.

6.4
1 I told my roommate to move out. **The last straw** was when she broke my favorite mug.
2 Sales **fell short of expectations** last month. We need to do better this month.
3 I know everyone else loves it, but this book is **not all that it's cracked up to be**.
4 I'm afraid this product just **isn't up to scratch**, Kyle.
5 His voice is OK, but he's **not going to set the world on fire**.

6.5
1 moth-eaten
2 a let-down
3 past its prime
4 second rate
5 cheap and nasty

07

7.2
A 6 B 3 C 5 D 2 E 1 F 4

7.3
1 It really gets my goat when someone eats smelly food on the train.
2 You're barking up the wrong tree if you think I can help you with your homework. I'm terrible at science.
3 Rachel always gets on her high horse about being a vegetarian. It's so annoying!
4 Bill looked like the cat that got the cream when he won the competition.
5 Our falling profits are the elephant in the room at every team meeting.

7.4
1 I tried to fix the photocopier, but I've really made a **pig's** ear of it.
2 My colleagues all have terrible colds. They're **dropping** like flies!
3 Ruby is a one-trick **pony**. She's a great singer, but she can't dance or act.
4 I **chickened** out of diving off the top board in the pool. It was too high!
5 Clarita's new apartment is tiny. There's not enough room to swing a **cat**.

7.5
1 gets my goat
2 not enough room to swing a cat
3 a bird's-eye view
4 a scaredy-cat
5 The world is your oyster.
6 like a deer in headlights

08

8.2
1 We're usually packed like sardines **on the bus to work in the morning.**
2 My granddaughter is the apple of my eye. **I'm so proud of her.**
3 We thought our walk would be really hilly, **but the land was as flat as a pancake.**
4 I felt warm and toasty **sitting in front of the fire.**
5 I don't like my job, **but it puts food on the table.**
6 You have to walk on eggshells around Dylan. **He gets upset so easily.**

8.3
1 I know Aiden's always late, but arriving late for his own wedding takes the cake!
2 I'm really stressed! I think I bit off more than I could chew when I took this promotion.
3 Fiona told me she doesn't like my new scooter. I think it's just sour grapes.
4 Asher is such a butterfingers. He is always dropping things.
5 Copies of Sadie's new novel are selling like hotcakes after it got great reviews.

8.4
1 B 2 C 3 A 4 B 5 A

8.5
1 eat humble pie
2 a couch potato
3 spoon-feeds
4 walk on eggshells
5 sugarcoat

09

9.4
1 My neighbor and I have **buried the hatchet** after arguing about the parking.
2 The negotiating teams stayed up all night **hammering out a deal**.
3 The government has **given the green light to** the construction of a new train station.
4 My girlfriend and I have **agreed to disagree** about what to do on vacation.

9.5
A 7 B 1 C 9 D 3 E 6 F 2 G 4
H 5 I 8

9.6
Hi Fiona,
How are you? I had some problems at work recently. My boss and I are usually on the same **page** about work, but we were at **odds** about my hours. She jumped down my **throat** when I said I couldn't work this weekend. We found the **middle** ground when I agreed to stay late on Friday.
See you soon,
Pablo

9.7
1 Diana and I reached a compromise about what movie to watch tonight.
2 Fran's dad gave her the thumbs-up to go out with her friends.
3 I tried to smooth things over between Pari and Toni after their argument.
4 Lenka and I fought like cats and dogs when we were children.
5 Samira has been given the go-ahead to play tennis after her injury.

9.8

1. held out an olive branch
2. on the same page
3. at odds
4. struck a deal
5. gave her the thumbs-up

10

10.5

1. Yoshiko offered a sympathetic ear when my cat went missing.
2. Aziz told me he'd crashed my car, but he was pulling my leg.
3. I was on my best behavior when I met my boyfriend's parents.
4. Pedro quit his job at the store, leaving me in the lurch.
5. Jean behaved out of character at the office party. She's normally so quiet!
6. Paulina poked fun at Mirek's new hairstyle.

10.6

GOOD BEHAVIOR:
generous to a fault
behaved beautifully
big hearted
lend a hand

BAD BEHAVIOR:
below the belt
treats them like dirt
let us down
unacceptable behavior

10.7

A 4 B 2 C 5 D 1 E 3

10.8

1. Henry can't control his **badly behaved** students.
2. I really **feel for** Mario. He has to work so hard in the kitchen.
3. My friends **ribbed me** for having such an old phone.
4. My dog **behaved beautifully** when I took him on the train.
5. Brad loves **playing practical jokes** on his brother.

11

11.4

1. I get **itchy feet** when I haven't been abroad for a long time.
2. Liz was **feeling blue** when her best friend left the country.
3. When Dylan copied her homework, Zoe was so angry that she was **foaming at the mouth**.
4. This terrible weather is **driving me nuts**.
5. My neighbor **saw red** when I parked in front of his house.

11.5

A 7 B 1 C 4 D 8 E 2 F 5 G 3 H 6

11.6

1. I was broken-hearted **when my girlfriend left me.**
2. I get itchy feet when I haven't **been abroad for a long time.**
3. Caitlin got cold feet **about singing karaoke.**
4. The children all went bananas **when I took them to the playground.**
5. My neighbor saw red **when I parked in front of his house.**

11.7

1. I **had egg on my face** after I called Jo's new boyfriend Ben. That was her ex-boyfriend's name!
2. After a long week at work, I **let my hair down** at my best friend's party.
3. Silvio went **as white as a sheet** when he got the bad news.
4. I was really upset when a customer shouted at me, but I managed to **keep a stiff upper lip**.
5. Leo **cried his eyes out** when I said he couldn't have another cookie.

12

12.5

1. The news that our profits were up was **music** to our ears.
2. Our new intern is such an **eager** beaver. She works really hard.
3. I was over the **moon** when I won the best actor award.
4. Salvador loves cooking. He puts his **heart** and soul into it.
5. I was on the edge of my **seat** as the detective revealed the murderer.

12.6

1. The kids **jumped for joy** when I brought our new puppy home.
2. Robbie has **flung himself into** training for the gymnastics competition.
3. My motorcycle is **my pride and joy**. I clean it every day.
4. Jamal **had butterflies in his stomach** as he waited for his date outside the restaurant.
5. Clara was **bright-eyed and bushy-tailed** as she set off on the hike.

12.7

1. The children were **bouncing off the walls** after a whole day indoors.
2. The news that our profits were up was **music to our ears**.
3. Jack was **on top of the world** when his team won the trophy.
4. I was **on the edge of my seat** as the detective revealed the murderer.
5. The sight of the park in spring is **a joy to behold**.

12.8

1. bursting with excitement
2. on cloud nine
3. head over heels
4. wept with joy
5. raring to go

13

13.5

1. Yannis was sad.
2. I was embarrassed.
3. I was sad.
4. I was afraid.
5. They were ashamed.

13.6

1 B 2 A 3 C 4 C 5 A

13.7

1. It makes my blood boil when people litter.
2. The sight of the old, spooky house made my hair stand on end.
3. Alice was shaking in her boots before she did her first bungee jump.
4. That horror movie sent shivers down my spine. It was so scary!

13.8

1. a downer
2. on the warpath
3. reduced to tears
4. that sinking feeling
5. wanted the earth to swallow her up
6. kicked myself

14

14.2

1. That boring lecture **went in one ear and out the other**!
2. I've seen that animal before, but **its name escapes me**.
3. Emi and Sofia **took a trip down memory lane** as they talked about their school days.
4. Jacob was explaining the diagram when he suddenly **lost his train of thought**.

14.3

1. You should keep in **mind** that it gets cold in the winter and pack some warm clothes.
2. The police showed me a photo of the suspect to jog my **memory**.

3 I enjoyed the party, but at the back of my **mind** I knew I had to catch the last train home.
4 Keeping busy at work is helping me erase the **memory** of my ex-girlfriend.

14.4
1 When the hotel receptionist asked me for my phone number, **my mind went blank**.
2 The answer to the teacher's question was **on the tip of my tongue**.
3 I'm sorry I didn't get you a present. **It slipped my mind** that it was your birthday.
4 I can't believe I forgot to bring the sandwiches! I've got **a memory like a sieve**.
5 **Memories are fading** of what the world was like before TV.

14.5
1 a photographic memory
2 memories came flooding back
3 racking my brain
4 rings a bell
5 erase the memory of
6 stirred up memories
7 in living memory
8 sprang to mind

15

15.2
1 burying his head in the sand
2 a bundle of nerves
3 getting on my nerves
4 Keep your chin up!
5 a shoulder to cry on
6 a pat on the back
7 has his heart set on

15.3
A 9 B 4 C 5 D 1 E 3 F 2 G 8
H 6 I 7

15.4
1 I hope the performance goes well, Adam. Break a leg!
2 Oh, no! I've forgotten my wallet. I'm such a scatterbrain!
3 Isla has such a sweet tooth. She loves eating cakes.
4 Wyatt is a good friend. He was a shoulder to cry on when I broke up with my girlfriend.

15.5
1 play it by ear
2 my heart sank
3 almost jumped out of his skin
4 has his heart set on
5 thick-skinned

15.6
1 Oh, no! I've forgotten my wallet. I'm such **a scatterbrain**!
2 When you're a parent, you need to **have eyes in the back of your head**!
3 Scarlett **got cold feet** about going on the rollercoaster.
4 There's nothing to do at work at the moment. I'm just sitting here **twiddling my thumbs**.
5 Maureen was **a bundle of nerves** before her wedding.

16

16.2
1 They were so angry with each other **that they almost came to blows!**
2 I decided to hold fire before **booking such an expensive holiday.**
3 The boss is in a terrible mood today! **We're all going to be in the line of fire.**
4 Poor you! **You've really been in the wars!**
5 I have some very bad news, **but please don't shoot the messenger!**

16.3
1 B 2 C 3 A 4 A 5 B

16.4
1 Balwant had to bite the **bullet** and tell his teacher that he hadn't done his homework.
2 Buying a house can be a **minefield**. There's always so much to think about!
3 I'm going to take my lunch break now. Could you hold down the **fort** until I get back?
4 Our daughter dropped a **bombshell** when she told us she and her new boyfriend were engaged.
5 Sonia stuck to her **guns** and told her daughter that she couldn't go to the party.

16.5
1 stabbed me in the back
2 an uphill battle
3 crossing swords
4 like a war zone
5 an ax to grind

17

17.3
1 a drop in the ocean
2 the middle of nowhere
3 everything but the kitchen sink
4 off the beaten path
5 in dribs and drabs
6 precious little

17.4
A 4 B 1 C 5 D 3 E 6 F 2

17.5
1 The guests began to arrive at the party **in dribs and drabs**.
2 My new apartment is **within walking distance** of my workplace.
3 We always take **everything but the kitchen sink** when we travel.
4 The castle is in **a far-flung corner** of the island. It takes hours to drive there.
5 Sharon lives in **the middle of nowhere**. You can't get there by train.

17.6
1 The Olympic swimming team has won tons of medals.
2 Carla's school is just a stone's throw away from the bus stop.
3 You don't need to drive to the store. It's just around the corner.
4 The forest stretched as far as the eye can see.

17.7
1 the middle of nowhere
2 far and wide
3 a thousand-and-one
4 few and far between
5 within walking distance
6 by a whisker
7 everything but the kitchen sink

18

18.4
1 My cake's going to be great. I'm just putting the **finishing** touches on it.
2 The pottery course was far too difficult for a **newbie** like me.
3 Mike's made a **fresh** start this year. He's eating much more healthily.
4 I've been marking tests all day, but the end is in **sight**!

18.5
1 beginning 2 ending 3 beginning
4 beginning 5 ending

18.6
1 Mia's fashion firm **got off to a flying start**. She has already won three awards.
2 It was **the end of an era** when our boss retired after 30 years.
3 After selling the last sandwich, Dean decided to **call it a day**.
4 Sophie's café finally **got off the ground** when she lowered her prices.
5 Trains across the city **ground to a halt** because of the snow.

18.7
1 a fitting end 2 call it a day 3 kicked off
4 get going 5 drew to a close

19

19.4

1 Rain is fairly likely.
2 Buster is likely to win.
3 It is very unlikely.
4 She is unlikely to pass.
5 It is almost certain.

19.5

1 I think Ruben's dreams of becoming a pop star are totally pie in the sky.
2 It looks like a medal is in the cards for Noriko after that amazing throw.
3 I'm afraid you're out of luck. The last train has just left the station.
4 We don't stand a chance of getting into the museum before lunchtime.
5 You're in luck! We have one dress left in your size.

19.6

1 It was just a case of **beginner's luck** when I won that card game. I'd never played it before.
2 There was only **a slim chance** that we'd see a cheetah, so we were amazed when we spotted one.
3 Russell has injured his knee. It's **touch-and-go** whether he'll be able to play in the tournament this month.
4 I hadn't studied for my tests, so it was **sheer luck** when I passed them.
5 I had an interview for a great job, but **blew it** when I arrived half an hour late.

19.7

1 on the off-chance
2 against all odds
3 a stroke of luck
4 Don't push your luck!
5 the hot favorite

20

20.3

A 3 B 5 C 4 D 1 E 2

20.4

1 There have been teething problems with the new computer system at work.
2 Unclogging my sink was a piece of cake for Carlita. She's a plumber.
3 Doing the dishes after a dinner party is a pain in the neck.
4 Getting around my city is a breeze. Our trains are excellent.
5 Finishing the building this month is going to be a tall order.

20.5

EASE:
smooth sailing
a breeze
like shooting fish in a barrel
with her eyes shut

DIFFICULTY:
easier said than done
out of his depth
a tall order
like getting blood from a stone

20.6

1 Don't **make a mountain out of a molehill**. I only asked you to help me bake a cake!
2 My home improvements **opened a can of worms**. The builders discovered so many problems.
3 The team has **a mountain to climb** if it wants to win the game.
4 I was **like a fish out of water** at the science fiction convention.
5 Doing the dishes after a dinner party is **a pain in the neck**.

21

21.3

1 Zahira is an excellent scuba teacher. You're **in safe hands** with her.
2 Hayley had **a close shave**. That ball almost hit her!
3 I advised Kathy not to go into the water. It would be **risking life and limb**.
4 The bear had left, and **the coast was clear**. We could continue with our trek.

21.4

1 safety 2 safety 3 danger 4 danger
5 safety 6 danger 7 safety 8 danger
9 danger

21.5

1 Maddy caught the train by the skin of her teeth. It left a few seconds later.
2 The rescue team found the climbers safe and sound after a week-long search.
3 You have to take your life in your hands every time you cross this road.
4 Make sure you wear a helmet when you're cycling! Remember, safety first!
5 The route through the jungle was fraught with danger.

21.6

1 in one piece
2 had a narrow escape
3 safety first
4 in safe hands
5 too close for comfort

22

22.3

1 a tough nut to crack
2 fighting a losing battle
3 rubbed salt into the wound
4 grin and bear it
5 thrown in at the deep end
6 pick up the pieces

22.4

B
D
E
G
I

22.5

1 Oh, no, I've missed the last bus home. I'm really in a **jam** now.
2 Working on the farm meant I had to come to **grips** with driving a tractor.
3 The peeling wallpaper was just the **tip** of the iceberg. The house needed so many repairs.
4 I hated working at the diner. The final **straw** was when they made me dress as a chicken.
5 The plumber got to the **bottom** of what's causing the leak. We need to replace the pipe.

22.6

1 Not being able to read music was **a stumbling block** when I started learning the saxophone.
2 The protesters want to stop the building being demolished, but they're **fighting a losing battle**.
3 If you let your children eat whatever they want for dinner, you're **making a rod for your own back**.
4 I hate going to the dentist, but I know I have to **grin and bear it**.
5 I can't believe you've upset your sister again! I'm the one who has to **pick up the pieces**.

22.7

1 a nightmare
2 a bumpy ride
3 in dire straits
4 a tough nut to crack
5 in a jam

23

23.4

1 What a scorcher! It's perfect weather for a barbecue.
2 We had to leave the beach because it started bucketing down.
3 Nina always takes her dog for a walk come rain or shine.

23.5

1 You weren't listening to me, were you? You had your head in the clouds.
2 This politician used to be really popular, but now the tide has turned.
3 Isaac and Fatima's argument about which movie to watch was just a storm in a teacup.
4 You don't need a coat, Phil! It's like an oven outside.
5 I'm so tired tonight! I'm going to hit the hay.
6 There are lots of cafés and restaurants in my neck of the woods.

23.6

1 a stick-in-the-mud
2 a ray of sunshine
3 take a rain check on
4 a breath of fresh air
5 a howling wind
6 like an oven
7 raining cats and dogs

23.7

A 2 B 5 C 4 D 1 E 7 F 8 G 3 H 6

24

24.3

1 I always enjoy a chitchat **with my sister over coffee.**
2 The students parroted the facts **without using their own words.**
3 Ahmed talks the talk, **but isn't very hardworking.**
4 I hate it when my boss **talks down to me!**
5 Leo can talk himself out **of any awkward situation.**
6 My colleagues love to talk shop **when they meet for lunch.**
7 This politician has a reputation **for speaking his mind.**
8 I made small talk with Marisha **while we waited for the train.**
9 I've tried telling Maya to clean up her room, **but it's like talking to a brick wall.**

24.4

1 talk shop
2 spins a good yarn
3 She can talk!
4 talk big
5 parroted
6 talks down to me
7 talks the talk

24.5

1 talk some sense into him
2 talk your ear off
3 a loudmouth
4 talks the talk

24.6

1 Nina keeps **droning on** about her new car. It's getting really boring!
2 This politician has a reputation for **speaking his mind**.
3 Sarah was born with **the gift of the gab**. She could sell you anything.
4 **Cat got your tongue?** You usually have so much to say.
5 I sat on the shore with my boyfriend, **shooting the breeze**.

25

25.4

A 5 B 7 C 1 D 6 E 4 F 2 G 8 H 3

25.5

1 We must have **got our wires crossed**. I thought the dress code for this party was casual.
2 When news stories are shocking, I always **take them with a grain of salt**.
3 The boss **stirred up a hornet's nest** when she said we would have to take a pay cut.
4 After leaving the band, Marco **dished the dirt** about the other band members to a journalist.
5 Anna's manager **touched base** with her for a quick update on her research.
6 The tour rep **broke the news** to us that our flight had been canceled.

25.6

1 I'm afraid your cat will have to stay here overnight, but I promise I'll keep you in the picture about how she's recovering.
2 Why did you spill the beans and tell Luke I had a new boyfriend? I wanted to tell him myself.
3 This restaurant couldn't afford an advertising campaign, but it has become really popular by word of mouth.
4 I'm planning a surprise trip to Paris with Liam to celebrate our wedding anniversary. Don't let the cat out of the bag!
5 Rumors that the two actors had secretly gotten married spread like wildfire.

25.7

1 the bearer of bad news
2 take them with a grain of salt
3 got our wires crossed
4 heard it through the grapevine
5 touched base

26

26.5

1 The children are being very quiet. I think there's something fishy going on!
2 Tania told me a secret but asked me to keep it under my hat.
3 My wife was angry when I went behind her back and bought myself a new motorcycle.
4 I promise I won't tell Lizzie you're going to propose to her. My lips are sealed.
5 I thought Bella's hat was ridiculous, but I told her a white lie and said I loved it.

26.6

TRUTH:
a whistleblower
came clean
above board
brutally honest

LIES:
bending the truth
telling half-truths
went behind her back
took us for a ride

26.7

A
C
D
G

26.8

Hi Sunita,
I have some exciting news for you, but please keep it **under** your hat because it's **top** secret at the moment. I've been promoted! I had a **hunch** that I would get the job because my interview went well. As I said, please don't tell anyone because my new boss still wants to keep it under **wraps**.
Love, Lindsay

26.9

1 I'm not going to tell you how much my house cost. It's **none of your business**!
2 **A whistleblower** has told the authorities about the dirty conditions in the kitchen at work.
3 I knew Frida hadn't been out sick. I **smelled a rat** when she came back to work with a suntan.
4 David **lied through his teeth** to his mom. He claimed the cat had broken her favorite vase.
5 My teacher was **brutally honest** with me and told me my essay was terrible.

27

27.3

1 Felipe **cast** a glance at his watch. The bus was already 10 minutes late.
2 Jenny, please tell me how the interview went. I'm all **ears**!
3 Bastian **kept** a close watch on his children as they played outside.
4 The examiner watched us like a **hawk**, making sure we didn't cheat.

5 Kezia looked furious when I told her I'd torn her dress. If **looks** could kill!
6 When my parents got **wind** of the fact that I'd had a house party, they were furious.
7 Omar lent a **sympathetic** ear when I broke up with my boyfriend.

27.4
A 3 B 1 C 9 D 4 E 2 F 8 G 6
H 5 I 7

27.5
1 If looks could kill!
2 hard of hearing
3 listening with half an ear
4 fell on deaf ears
5 cast an eye over
6 watched us like a hawk
7 lent a sympathetic ear
8 turned a blind eye

27.6
1 Be careful what you say about the boss. Remember, walls have ears!
2 We kept our eyes peeled, hoping we'd spot some rare birds.
3 Martina didn't hear the teacher's question. She was a million miles away.
4 The border guard gave my documents the once-over, then let me drive on.
5 The teacher turned a blind eye to his students' bad behavior.

27.7
1 music to my ears
2 an eagle eye
3 cast an eye over
4 fell on deaf ears
5 hard of hearing

28

28.2
1 face the music
2 changed your tune
3 jazz up
4 The show must go on!
5 fine-tune
6 get the show on the road
7 read him like a book

28.3
1 Antonio is great at flower arranging. He **has it down to an art**.
2 Juanita is so careful at work. She **does everything by the book**.
3 I'm going to **take a page out of your book** and clean my desk.
4 The police chief **put us in the picture** about the bank robbery.
5 How many times must I **drum it into your head**? Wipe your feet on the mat!

28.4
1 toot her own horn
2 music to my ears
3 drum up
4 made a scene
5 is like a broken record
6 face the music

28.5
1 Ian's desserts are amazing. He'll be **a tough act to follow** when he leaves.
2 Arjun felt **left out of the picture** when his roommates got a dog without telling him.
3 You've **changed your tune**! I thought you didn't like cats.
4 Nisha is helping me **fine-tune** my presentation for tomorrow morning.
5 Dennis broke his mom's laptop. He had to **face the music** and tell her.

29

29.3
1 We sat in front of the TV stuffing our faces with popcorn.
2 Nigel took a tray of piping hot cupcakes out of the oven.
3 Ethan took his new client out for a sit-down meal.
4 You shouldn't eat so many cookies! You'll spoil your appetite.
5 Aliyah whipped up an omelet for Caleb and his friends.
6 Mario celebrated his 70th birthday with a feast fit for a king.
7 I washed down my pizza with a glass of lemonade.
8 We complained to the waiter that our soup was stone cold.

29.4
1 C 2 B 3 C 4 B 5 C

29.5
1 Mario celebrated his 70th birthday with **a feast fit for a king**.
2 I was in a rush, so I **grabbed something to eat** from the fast food stand.
3 The sight of the cake in the café window **made my mouth water**.
4 Chris bought **a round of drinks** for the basketball team.
5 I'm so glad I ordered an extra-large pizza. **I could eat a horse!**

29.6
1 a square meal
2 eats like a bird
3 wolfed down
4 whipped up
5 spoil your appetite

30

30.3
1 I don't feel very well. I think I'm **coming down with something**.
2 Moving to the country has given Kira **a new lease on life**.
3 Ollie received **a clean bill of health** from his doctor.
4 The dancers in this show have to be **as fit as a fiddle**.

30.4
1 health 2 sickness 3 sickness 4 health
5 sickness 6 sickness 7 health 8 sickness
9 sickness

30.5
1 This music's far too loud! It has given me **a splitting headache**.
2 A week at a health spa was **just what the doctor ordered** after a stressful month at work.
3 Uma is **up and about** following her operation last week.
4 Imran looks **the picture of health** since he started going to the gym.
5 A relaxing afternoon in the park helped me **recharge my batteries**.

30.6
1 the worse for wear
2 throwing up
3 on the mend
4 in bad shape
5 flare up
6 a heavy cold
7 get in shape

31

31.4
1 Brad thought he would pass the test easily, **but he only scraped by.**
2 Our cutting-edge products **have made our company millions of dollars.**
3 The professor's astrophysics lecture **went over my head.**
4 Ian is such a bookworm. **He loves reading.**
5 Vineetha loves modern art. **She knows it inside out.**
6 Ping's design for the new library **really breaks the mold.**
7 These doctors have made **a breakthrough in their medical research.**

31.5
1 We both thought of buying Dan a camera for his birthday. **Great minds think alike!**
2 Dion's new laptop is **light-years ahead of** his old one.

3 Ben accused Stefan of being **a copycat**. Their artworks were very similar.
4 Mary's an expert in ancient history. She really **knows her stuff**.
5 The professor's astrophysics lecture **went over my head**.

31.6
1 Andrea only started work here last week. She's till learning the **ropes**.
2 I can show you around my city. I know it like the **back** of my hand.
3 My client wanted a completely new design. I had to put on my thinking **cap**.
4 I just can't make heads or **tails** of this map.
5 Peter's **brushing** up on his French before his vacation in Paris.

31.7
1 scraped by
2 state-of-the-art
3 a copycat
4 a bookworm
5 can't make heads or tails of
6 a breakthrough
7 passed with flying colors

32

32.2
1 I loved looking after Nadia's cat while she was on vacation. It was easy money.
2 Vegetables don't have to be expensive. Carrots and cabbage are dirt cheap at this store.
3 My daughter wants a new smartphone. I keep telling her money doesn't grow on trees!
4 It was really generous of Imran to buy us dinner at that expensive restaurant, but he does like to throw money around.

32.3
CHEAP:
dirt cheap
rock-bottom prices
cost next to nothing

EXPENSIVE:
a hefty sum
pricey
a rip-off

32.4
1 tighten his belt
2 saved for a rainy day
3 out of pocket
4 struck it rich
5 rolling in it

32.5
A 4 B 6 C 1 D 3 E 2 F 5

32.6
1 I found it hard to **make ends meet** when I was a student, so I started working in a café.
2 Aranza and Dominic decided to **go Dutch** at the end of the meal.
3 Luna wants to buy a house soon, so she's building up **a nest-egg**.
4 Marco had to **tighten his belt**, so he started bringing his own lunch to work.
5 Getting the car fixed will be expensive, but luckily I have **saved for a rainy day**.

33

33.2
CHEAP:
a good deal
bargain-basement prices
slash prices

EXPENSIVE:
highway robbery
cost an arm and a leg
pay over the odds

33.3
A 9 B 4 C 3 D 7 E 1 F 5 G 6 H 2 I 8

33.4
1 He looks for cheap things.
2 The jacket was cheap.
3 They reduce prices a lot.
4 Ayesha doesn't buy anything.
5 They bought lots of things.

33.5
1 My new suit cost an arm and a leg. I bought it from a tailor in Milan.
2 After winning the lottery, Tomás went on a shopping spree.
3 The taxi from the airport cost more than $70. It was highway robbery!
4 Austin needed some retail therapy, so he spent the afternoon at the mall.
5 This store sells designer labels at bargain-basement prices.
6 Javier drove a hard bargain, refusing to drop the price of his house.

33.6
1 splurge
2 shop around
3 pay over the odds
4 slash prices
5 cost a fortune

34

34.3
1 get a move on
2 from dusk till dawn
3 once in a blue moon
4 before we knew it
5 at the crack of dawn

34.4
B
D
E
G
H

34.5
1 Time's **up**! I need you to give me an answer now.
2 The teacher told Cory to stop **wasting** time on his phone.
3 I was woken in the **dead** of night by a loud noise outside.
4 We were up at the **crack** of dawn to catch our flight.
5 That meeting really **dragged** on. Colm was almost asleep by the end.

34.6
1 before we knew it
2 the wee hours
3 Time's up!
4 a drag
5 in the nick of time
6 flown by

34.7
1 Júlio **took his time** finishing his painting. He wanted it to be perfect.
2 Victoria is always **on time** for her English class.
3 Ren arrived **bright and early** for his first day at work.
4 It's nearly midnight. It's **about time** we went home.
5 Huan only cooks at home **once in a blue moon**.

35

35.2
1 We need to roll up our sleeves **if we're going to finish painting the house today.**
2 If Gavin doesn't start working harder, **we'll have to give him the boot.**
3 Austin is in a lot of trouble. **I wouldn't want to be in his shoes.**
4 My boss got very hot under the collar **when I handed my report in late.**
5 The movie was a spy thriller **with lots of cloak-and-dagger action.**
6 If Sven wins the race, **I'll eat my hat!**

7. My daughter thinks my taste **in music is really old hat.**
8. Jane has a bee in her bonnet **about people dropping litter on the sidewalk**.

35.3

1. Pedro's upset about failing the test. You'll have to **handle him with kid gloves**.
2. Ian's become **too big for his boots** since his promotion. He always ignores me.
3. When Juan won the national art prize, it was **a feather in his cap**.
4. My teacher explained that I would fail my exam if I didn't **pull my socks up**.

35.4

1. This steak really is **as tough as shoe leather**. I need a sharper knife!
2. My cousin is very emotional. He'll start an argument **at the drop of a hat**.
3. Carter is such **a clever clogs**. He's always the first to raise his hand in class.
4. After working at the bank for 30 years, it was time for me to **hang up my boots**.
5. We need to **roll up our sleeves** if we're going to finish painting the house today.

35.5

1. give him the boot
2. up my sleeve
3. in his shoes
4. roll up our sleeves
5. hang up my boots
6. off-the-cuff
7. lining her pockets
8. old hat

36

36.4

1 B 2 A 3 B 4 C 5 A

36.5

1. She's working hard.
2. We rested.
3. Julie tried her best.
4. Carmen is not working hard.
5. It was hard work.

36.6

1. Leo always goes the extra mile to keep our customers happy.
2. Akash usually takes 40 winks after he's finished his lunch.
3. I'm sorry, I can't talk to you for long. I have my hands full.
4. Celia had to put her head down and finish her essay to meet the deadline.
5. Brandon is a slacker. He looks at his phone all day and ignores the customers.
6. After a long day working at the store, Marc likes to put his feet up and watch TV.

36.7

1. pulled out all the stops
2. roll up our sleeves
3. snowed under
4. elbow grease
5. didn't lift a finger

37

37.2

1. The client hates my design for the company logo, so **it's back to the drawing board**.
2. The traffic usually moves **at a snail's pace** during the rush hour.
3. The guests **made a beeline for** all the cakes on the table.
4. Scientists are **on the verge of** developing intelligent robots.

37.3

A 3 B 5 C 1 D 2 E 4

37.4

1. begin a trip or a drive
2. open and working well
3. back to the beginning
4. not making any progress
5. made a lot of progess

37.5

1. The hikers **forged ahead** in spite of the terrible snowstorm.
2. I'm **running around like a headless chicken** trying to get the meal ready for my guests tonight.
3. **Slowly but surely**, my daughter is learning to ride a bike.
4. I was late for my business meeting, so I had to eat lunch **on the run**.
5. The children threw the ball **back and forth** as they played outside.

38

38.3

1. a slap on the wrist
2. broke the law
3. twisted her arm
4. reached a verdict
5. calls the shots

38.4

1. It was the day of reckoning. The judge was about to sentence Mason for burglary.
2. It's important to obey the law when you're cycling in the city.
3. It's the children who rule the roost in Kaylee's family. They don't respect her.
4. Ben suffered the consequences of his misbehavior and had to wash the car.
5. Seth took the law into his own hands and confronted the vandals.

38.5

1. Carla refused to **toe the line** and wear the same uniform as the other students.
2. Jack's boss is always **breathing down his neck**. He wants more independence.
3. The party **got out of hand**, so the neighbors called the police.
4. Since leaving jail, Crystal has **kept on the straight and narrow**.
5. Pedro's father **put his foot down** and refused to let him watch TV.

38.6

1. let him off the hook
2. reached a verdict
3. twisted her arm
4. the head
5. calls the shots
6. a slap on the wrist

39

39.3

SUCCESS:
hit the big time
worked like a charm
brought the house down

FAILURE:
on the ropes
go sideways
screwed up

39.4

1. The gang's plan to rob the bank **went belly up** when a policeman recognized Mike.
2. Nicola's decision to take her dog shopping turned out to be **a recipe for disaster**.
3. Nathan's first book was **an overnight success**. It sold a million copies in a month.
4. Lucy's beauty salon is **going from strength to strength**. She's opening another soon.
5. Margaret's performance **fell flat on its face**. She can't sing!

39.5

1 success 2 failure 3 failure 4 success
5 failure 6 success 7 success 8 success
9 failure

39.6

1. won it hands down
2. go sideways
3. an overnight success
4. brought the house down
5. fell flat on its face
6. going from strength to strength

7 a recipe for disaster
8 hit the jackpot
9 screwed up

40

40.3

1 Andrew made sure he **had his ducks in a row** before his presentation.
2 Maya is a great designer. She always **thinks outside the box**.
3 Irena's internship at the fashion firm helped her to get **a foot in the door**.
4 We're **working around the clock** to make sure the new subway line opens on time.

40.4

A 5 B 3 C 7 D 6 E 1 F 4 G 8 H 2

40.5

1 Carlos has lots of **hands-on** experience working with horses.
2 Sara has handed in her **notice** at work. She's going to study engineering.
3 After studying for many years, Anna embarked on a **career** as a surgeon.
4 I'm really bored at work, so I've decided to start job **hunting**.
5 Rory goes the extra **mile** to make sure his customers are satisfied.

40.6

1 landed a job
2 in a nutshell
3 tied up
4 goes the extra mile
5 fired

41

41.5

1 I've decided to leave the rat race **and move to the country.**
2 My dad had a blue-collar job **in the construction industry.**
3 We decided to blacklist this supplier **after they sent us faulty products.**
4 After many years in journalism, **Simon became a big cheese in the media.**
5 There's a lot of red tape involved **in health and safety in the warehouse.**

41.6

1 We ask all our interview candidates the same questions to create **a level playing field**.
2 Our range of cereal is **a cash cow**. It's cheap to make and customers love it.
3 I have **a white-collar job** in an investment bank.
4 Our new bags are **selling like hotcakes**. We need to order more.
5 Evan is always asking me what to do. I feel like I have to **spoon-feed** him.

41.7

1 We ask all our interview candidates the same questions to create **a level playing field**.
2 Emily is **a team player**. She works so well with all her colleagues at the bookstore.
3 Our boss is leaving the restaurant soon, and Angela is **the front-runner** to get his job.
4 We've already reduced our price by 25 percent. **The ball is in your court.**
5 I play in a band every weekend, but teaching guitar is **my bread and butter**.
6 Boris was given **a golden handshake** when he retired from the company.

41.8

1 in the red
2 bring home the bacon
3 the lion's share
4 the top dog
5 a white-collar job

42

42.2

1 All our gardeners are really hardworking, but Hannah is in a league of her own.
2 This client keeps moving the goalposts. Now she wants the bedroom painted red.
3 We don't have enough time to train our employees properly. They'll just have to sink or swim.
4 We've got a lot of unpacking to do, so let's get the ball rolling.
5 I often have to work evenings, but I knew the score when I decided to accept this job.

42.3

1 cleared a hurdle
2 in full swing
3 a ballpark figure
4 par for the course
5 below par
6 on the ball
7 get the ball rolling

42.4

1 the gloves are off
2 at this stage of the game
3 thrown in at the deep end
4 saved by the bell
5 threw us a curveball

42.5

1 The firefighters **tackled** the fire at the warehouse and made sure everyone got out safely.
2 I've had cats and rabbits before, but looking after a dog is **a whole new ball game**.
3 The plumber gave us **a ballpark figure** for the cost of the new bathroom.
4 I'm sorry you didn't get through to the next round, Cameron. **You win some, you lose some!**
5 I've failed my driving test for the tenth time. I think it's time to **throw in the towel**.

43

43.3

1 Doug is **making** progress on his new novel and hopes to finish it soon.
2 I want to get fit, so I've started **doing** exercise every day.
3 **Do** your best in the game today! I know you can beat the other team.
4 There's something wrong with the photocopier. It's **making** a strange noise.
5 I always **do** my homework as soon as I get home from school.
6 The children had fun painting, but they've really **made** a mess.
7 Can you **do** me a favor and get that book down from the shelf?

43.4

1 Zoe did her hair before her best friend's engagement party.
2 I made a phone call to our client in India to discuss some important business.
3 I was quite offended when Laura made a joke about my new sweater.
4 The flood did a lot of damage to our house, so we had to move out.
5 We did an experiment in the laboratory as part of our research project.

43.5

A 5 B 8 C 1 D 4 E 7 F 3 G 6 H 2

43.6

1 I **made** some friends from the local area while I was on vacation.
2 I always **do** my homework as soon as I get home from school.
3 We're **making** arrangements for our summer vacation in Italy.
4 I was really pleased when Sue **made** a cake for my birthday.
5 We **did** an experiment in the laboratory as part of our research project.
6 I was quite offended when Laura **made** a joke about my new sweater.
7 The flood **did** a lot of damage to our house, so we had to move out.
8 I want to get fit, so I've started **doing** exercise every day.
9 My daughter always **makes** her bed in the morning.
10 Can you **do** me a favor and get that book down from the shelf?

44

44.3

GIVE:
a presentation
an example
the impression
birth
a speech
priority
me a hug
an answer

TAKE:
a photo
a chance
a nap
a bite
a shower
a seat
the lead
a look

44.4

1 Dwayne likes to take a shower as soon as he gets home from work.
2 Emily is giving a presentation about the company's sales figures.
3 Hamid took a photo of his class in front of the Colosseum.
4 Near the end of the race, Axel passed the other athletes and took the lead.

44.5

1 I had a big suitcase, so Selma offered **to give me a lift to the airport.**
2 The dog gave the impression **that he wanted to go out for a walk.**
3 Mario and I are taking **a drawing class this evening.**
4 The receptionist asked me to take **a seat while I waited for the hairdresser.**
5 Drivers should always give **priority to pedestrians.**

44.6

A 3 B 1 C 4 D 2 E 6 F 5 G 7

44.7

1 When Danny got to the hotel, he **gave** me a call to say he had arrived safely.
2 Hamid **took** a photo of his class in front of the Colosseum.
3 The professor **gave** a speech to the students about her new discovery.
4 Emily is **giving** a presentation about the company's sales figures.
5 Dwayne likes to **take** a shower as soon as he gets home from work.

45

45.3

1 After gardening all morning, we were so tired that we needed to have a rest.
2 I need to go to bed now. I'm getting tired.
3 Shreya's going to have a baby this summer.
4 Michael and Heather had an argument about the rules of the game.
5 Lily had a conversation with another passenger on the train.

45.4

A 3 B 4 C 1 D 2 E 8 F 5 G 7 H 6

45.5

1 Robin always **gets angry** when his children refuse to eat their food.
2 I **have an appointment** to see the vet at 2 o'clock this afternoon.
3 Sean and Lisa **had a talk** about the new design for the office.
4 Tiffany **had fun** at the festival with her friends.

45.6

1 Kylie **had a party** to celebrate her 18th birthday. It was great fun!
2 Claude is **getting better** at making cakes.
3 I need to go to bed now. I'm **getting tired**.
4 After gardening all morning, we were so tired that we needed to **have a rest**.
5 You really need to **get going** if you want to catch the train.

46

46.3

A 3 B 1 C 5 D 2 E 4

46.4

1 Catalina has set the date for her wedding next summer.
2 After telling my boss I was leaving my job, I put it in writing.
3 I set homework for my students at the end of every lesson.
4 I had a long way to drive, so I set off nice and early.

46.5

1 put her cards on the table
2 put off
3 put a stop to
4 put me in charge of
5 put it bluntly

46.6

1 I really **put** my foot in it when I asked if Hazel was Tamsin's mother. They are actually sisters.
2 Judy was sad to see the birds trapped in their cage, so she **set** them free.
3 The ship **set** sail for China this morning. It will arrive in 20 days.
4 Terry **puts** his family first. He always leaves work in time to meet his children after school.
5 Sakura has been **putting** the heat on the contractors to finish the job quickly.

46.7

1 Silvio called the fire department **after he accidentally set fire to his shed.**
2 After telling my boss I was leaving my job, **I put it in writing.**
3 I had a long way to drive, **so I set off nice and early.**
4 I always put off doing my homework **until the last minute.**
5 Ed set the table **before his guests arrived for dinner.**
5 Irfan has put me in charge of **the store while he is on vacation**.

47

47.3

GO:
bankrupt
quiet
abroad
fishing
deaf
crazy
missing
bad

COME:
to a standstill
close
to a decision
into view
to an agreement
in last
prepared
to the rescue

47.4

1 Riya came prepared for the camping trip.
2 When the play came to an end, everyone left the theater.
3 My kids go crazy whenever they hear that song.
4 That style of shirt went out of fashion years ago!

47.5

A 4 B 1 C 3 D 2 E 6 F 5

47.6

1 This fruit has **gone** bad. It's not good to eat.
2 My aunt's **going** deaf. You'll have to speak more loudly.
3 The judges have **come** to a decision about the winner.

4 Sara's fashion boutique **went** bankrupt. She couldn't afford the rent.
5 Everyone **went** quiet when the boss walked into the room.
6 My move **went** smoothly. I had lots of people helping me.
7 The team has **come** to an agreement about which logo design to use.

47.7

1 Joshua's dog has **gone missing**. He's putting up signs around town.
2 We were stranded on the rocks until the lifeguards **came to the rescue**.
3 Dougie prefers to **go abroad** on vacation.
4 Pavel likes to **go fishing** on Saturdays.
5 Paula trained very hard and **came in first** in the hurdles.

48

48.5

1 Two firefighters **paid** a visit to my son's school today to talk about fire safety.
2 I'm trying to call the bank and they've asked me to **hold** the line. It's so annoying!
3 Cleo told me about her mom's surprise party but asked me to **keep** it a secret.
4 We **hold** a meeting each Monday to discuss the week ahead.

48.6

1 catch his eye
2 caught the train
3 caught a cold
4 catch my breath
5 catch fire

48.7

1 B 2 B 3 C 4 A

48.8

1 The teacher asked the students **to keep quiet during the test.**
2 The children paid close attention to John **as he told them about his travels.**
3 I live with my parents, but **pay my way by buying groceries.**
4 Natalie always keeps calm **when she has to talk to angry customers.**
5 After climbing the stairs, **I stopped to catch my breath.**
6 Pari usually drives to work, **but she caught the train this morning.**
7 Raul caught a glimpse of **a deer as he hiked through the forest.**
8 Kelly paid me a compliment **and said she liked my new haircut.**

48.9

1 pay you back
2 paid tribute
3 hold my tongue
4 hold the line
5 paid me a compliment
6 holds a grudge
7 paid close attention

49

49.7

1 André gets up **ridiculously early** every morning.
2 This food is **absolutely delicious**. You're such a good cook!
3 We **strongly advise** you not to travel unless it is absolutely necessary.
4 That date was **unbelievably awkward**. We had nothing to say to each other.
5 Gina was **deeply concerned** when her cat didn't come home for his dinner.

49.8

1 Cesar's new movie was **highly praised by the critics.**
2 The park is absolutely beautiful **at this time of year.**
3 I was deeply hurt when Madison **didn't invite me to her wedding.**
4 The portions in this restaurant **are ridiculously small.**
5 Malachi strongly believes in **looking after the environment.**

49.9

ABSOLUTELY:
delicious
useless
fantastic

HIGHLY:
unlikely
probable
praised

RIDICULOUSLY:
easy
expensive
early

STRONGLY:
believes
feels
advise

49.10

1 I was **unbelievably** lucky to get my violin back after I left it on the train.
2 Gina was **deeply** concerned when her cat didn't come home for his dinner.
3 I **highly** recommend this book. I stayed up all night reading it!
4 Some people can be **unbelievably** selfish when they are on the bus.
5 Malachi **strongly** believes in looking after the environment.

50

50.4

1 I don't need help carrying my bag. It's as light as a **feather**.
2 My uncle is as strong as an **ox**. He's a champion weightlifter.
3 My grandfather is as **wise** as an owl. He always gives good advice.
4 I'm as blind as a **bat** without my glasses.
5 Paul is as quiet as a **mouse**. He never talks in meetings.

50.5

1 There was no rain for months, and the land was **as dry as a bone**.
2 Fiona looked **as proud as a peacock** in her new hat.
3 Mary's car is **as old as the hills**. She refuses to buy a new one.
4 Selma **slept like a log** after a long day climbing in the Alps.

50.6

1 as good as gold
2 as deaf as a post
3 shaking like a leaf
4 as white as a sheet
5 as fast as lightning
6 as brave as a lion

50.7

A
C
E
G
H

50.8

1 Have you been out in the snow? Your hands are **as cold as ice**!
2 Mary's car is **as old as the hills**. She refuses to buy a new one.
3 Javier was **as busy as a bee** getting ready for the party.
4 Roy's new suit **fits like a glove**. He looks really good.
5 My grandmother is **as deaf as a post**. She always turns up the TV really loud.

51

51.2

1 Honesty is the best policy.
2 Many hands make light work.
3 There's no time like the present.
4 Two heads are better than one.
5 Curiosity killed the cat.
6 Better late than never.
7 Actions speak louder than words.

51.3

A 2 B 5 C 4 D 9 E 7 F 1 G 8
H 3 I 6

51.4

1 **Don't count your chickens before they hatch**, Kim! The game isn't over yet.
2 Stop sitting by the phone waiting to hear if you got the job. **A watched pot never boils.**
3 I've been playing the trumpet every day and I'm really improving. **Practice makes perfect.**
4 Azra adores her pet snake. I suppose **beauty is in the eye of the beholder**.

51.5

1 Flo's incompetence at work is affecting the whole team. A chain is only as strong as its weakest link.
2 We're almost ready for the party and we've still got plenty of time. Many hands make light work.
3 The day the sales began, Tamsin was outside the store at 6 in the morning. The early bird catches the worm!
4 Jakob really misses his girlfriend now that she has gone to college. Absence makes the heart grow fonder.
5 You were meant to give me this assignment a week ago, but better late than never.

51.6

1 Better late than never.
2 Honesty is the best policy.
3 Curiosity killed the cat.
4 Actions speak louder than words.

52

52.8

1 Yes, I will **lend** you my laptop, but please be careful with it.
2 I **expect** that there will be lots of people at the party.
3 I **hope** I still get into college.
4 Suddenly, Jules **heard** a loud bang coming from behind him.
5 This pie that you've been baking **smells** delicious!

52.9

1 Jules often **listens to** music on his walk home from work.
2 Come outside and **look at** the flowers I planted last month.
3 The Lions have **won** the soccer championship again.
4 The Lions **beat** the Stars 3–1.
5 I **saw** Keiko's large ginger cat lying on the lawn.

52.10

1 The cat watched the birds **sitting in a tree.**
2 I wish my **test results were better.**
3 This pie that you've been baking **smells delicious!**
4 Suddenly, Jules heard a loud bang **coming from behind him.**
5 I expect that there will be **lots of people at the party.**
6 Come outside and look at **the flowers I planted last month.**
7 The Lions have won **the soccer championship again.**
8 I'm really looking forward to **seeing the fireworks display at the party.**
9 Jules often listens to **music on his walk home from work.**

52.11

A 6 B 3 C 1 D 8 E 5 F 7 G 4 H 2

53

53.8

1 "Oh, no," said Kayleigh. "I've left my school bag on the bus with all my homework in it."
2 Colm injured his foot when he dropped the vase.
3 There is lots of work to do. I have to stack shelves and serve customers.
4 Are you sure you want to buy that car? It would be more sensible to save your money.

53.9

1 Colm's foot still hurt for days after the accident.
2 Wait a minute! I need to charge my phone before we go.
3 Silvia reminded Sanjay to visit his mother on her birthday.
4 I have a job as a sales assistant in a supermarket.

53.10

A 4 B 2 C 7 D 3 E 8 F 6 G 1 H 5

53.11

1 There's no need to be so **sensitive**! I was only trying to give you advice.
2 Kayleigh had to **tell** her teacher that she had left her homework on the bus.
3 Colm **damaged** Sheila's vase when he dropped it.
4 Sanjay **remembered** to visit his mother, who was delighted to see him.
5 Nina **wore** her new dress to Jack's party.
6 Don't forget to bring water. I'll **fill up** some bottles for us.

54

54.2

1 a red-letter day
2 pitch black
3 the green belt
4 a black eye
5 turned beet-red
6 a black-tie event
7 a green thumb

54.3

Hi Sandra,
Alyssa knocked on my door out of the **blue** yesterday. I hadn't seen her for years! She said she was going to paint the town **red** for her birthday next week, and invited me along, too. You know I only go out once in a **blue** moon, so I thought it would be a **golden** opportunity to meet some new friends. She said I could bring a friend along. Would you like to come with me?
Love,
Janice

54.4

1 Sergio got **a black eye** after he walked into a lamppost.
2 The actress made her first appearance **on the silver screen** in the 1950s.
3 I always **get the blues** when my vacation is over and I have to go back to work.
4 The boys were **caught red-handed** when they tried to break into the house.

54.5

1 I thought my new boss was really nice, but he showed his true colors when I forgot to put sugar in his coffee.
2 Fake designer goods are sold on the black market.
3 There's a gray area in the office dress code. My boss said it was casual, but she told me I couldn't wear shorts.
4 I want to be a teacher, so getting work experience at the school was a golden opportunity for me.
5 We're protesting against plans to build houses on the green belt in our local area.

54.6

1 black and blue
2 saw red
3 a green thumb
4 green with envy
5 out of the blue

Index of idioms and expressions

Numbers refer to the module number.

C

D

E

F

G

H

I

M

N

O

P

Q

R

S

T

W

Y

Z

Index of common words and subjects

Entries are listed by unit number or module number. Main entries are **bold**.

Acknowledgments

The publisher would like to thank:

Edward Aves for editorial assistance; Shahid Mahmood, Chhaya Sajwan, and Michelle Staples for design assistance; Steph Lewis for proofreading and indexing; Christine Stroyan for audio recording management; and ID Audio for audio recording and production.